D0966917

Presented To

_____

On

_____

By

_____

LIFE ON PURPOSE™ DEVOTIONAL

*Practical Faith and Profound Insight
for Every Day*

By
J.M. Farro

Harrison House
Tulsa, OK

07 06 05 04   10 9 8 7 6 5 4 3 2 1

Life on Purpose™ *Devotional:*
Practical Faith and Profound Insight for Every Day
ISBN 1-57794-650-2
Copyright © 2004 by J.M. Farro
P.O. Box 434
Nazareth, PA 18064

Published by Harrison House, Inc.
P.O. Box 35035
Tulsa, OK 74153

Contents

Try God

{ *Oh, put God to the test and see how kind he is! See for yourself the way his mercies shower down on all who trust in him!* }

PSALM 34:8 TLB

Eleven years ago my life was in such turmoil that I can still recall sitting in front of the television desperately searching for answers to my problems. I knew my relationship with my husband wasn't what it should be. There was a lot of tension between us much of the time, and there were ever-present undercurrents of distrust and resentment. My sons were in the early stages of their teen years, and my older son was already showing serious signs of rebellion. I was constantly struggling with anxiety and depression, as well as a feeling of emptiness that threatened to consume me. As waves of despair swept over me, I flipped the channel to hear a fiery man of God speak words that changed my life forever. He said, "You've tried everything else—now try God!" I *had* tried everything else. I had read and listened to everything the "experts" had to say about having a happy marriage, raising well-adjusted children, and living a contented and fulfilled life. And I was miserable. I was ready to try anything—even God. Then I heard the TV preacher say, "Take God at His Word and watch Him work miracles in your life!" I made a commitment to the Lord that day to believe, study, and apply His Word to my life from that moment on. As I began to cry tears of sorrow, regret, and repentance, I prayed, "Lord, I've made a mess out of my life, and I ask You to forgive me in Jesus' name. I give my life to You, and I ask that You make it into something new and wonderful, for Your glory." Since I prayed that simple, heart-felt prayer, my life has never been the same. My family and I have had our trials and troubles along the way, but I can testify that this promise of His is true: "The good man does not escape all troubles—he has them too. But the Lord helps him in each and every one"! (Ps. 34:29 TLB).

One of the life-changing truths I learned as I began seriously studying the Bible is that God wants me to enjoy my life. For years, I had believed that I shouldn't expect too much out of life and that I should just be satisfied with my lot. But then I read the Savior's words in John 10:10 in the Amplified Bible: "The thief comes only in order to steal and kill and destroy. I came that they may have and *enjoy* life, and have it in abundance (to the full, till it overflows)." I finally realized that God didn't want me to settle for a life of mediocrity and misery. He didn't want me to just survive—He wanted me to thrive! And He sent His Son to model the abundant life for me so that I could follow His example. As I studied the Scriptures, I also learned that I have a very powerful and evil enemy—Satan, who comes only to "steal, kill and destroy."

LIVE ON PURPOSE TODAY

Purpose to stop being an easy mark for the devil through ignorance of the Bible.
Take some extra time today to look up Scriptures in God's Word that declare who God intends you to be.

Even though I had been a Christian since I was very young, I never had a working knowledge of God's Word. In Mark 12:24, Jesus says, "Are you not in error because you do not know the Scriptures or the power of God?" My ignorance of the Scriptures made me an easy target for the devil's deceptions, and as a result, he had a tremendous influence over my life. As I devoted myself to God and His Word, I began to discover the truth that set me free from my bondages (John 8:32) and that opened the door to the fulfillment of His precious promises. I also learned to apply Proverbs 3:5-6 to every area of my life: "Trust in the Lord with all your heart; do not depend on your own understanding. Seek His will in all you do, and He will direct your paths." I stopped relying on my own wisdom and reasoning, and I began seeking God's wisdom and direction in every matter that concerned me and my family. The more I put my trust in God and His Word, the more peace, joy, and success I experienced. I've tried living my way, and I've tried living God's way, and today I'm living proof that God's ways are best. If you aren't enjoying the abundant life that Jesus came to give you, I pray you'll "put God to the test and see how kind He is! See for yourself the way His mercies shower down on all who trust in Him"! (Ps. 34:8 TLB).

PRAYER

Lord, today I surrender my whole life to You. I ask that You transform all my troubles into triumphs, for Your glory. Help me to spend time in Your presence daily through prayer and Bible study so that You can impart Your truth to me. Thank You that as I trust in You and seek Your will, You'll direct me in the paths of Your greatest blessings!

How God's Word Ensures Our Victory

Do not let this Book of the Law depart from your mouth; meditate on it day and night, so that you may be careful to do everything written in it. Then you will be prosperous and successful.

JOSHUA 1:8

These verses contain some of the instructions God gave Joshua as he was about to step into Moses' shoes as leader of the Israelites. It's interesting to note that as part of Joshua's preparation, the Lord commanded him to constantly meditate on His Word and keep it on his lips. God is teaching us a very important lesson here. As we face the various challenges of our daily lives, we need to continually dwell on God's truths and promises. As long as we are living on this earth, we will be exposed to worldly ways and Satan's deception on a regular basis. Only by renewing our minds, as Paul instructs us in Romans 12:2, can we resist and overcome ungodly influences. How do we renew our minds? With the Word of God. We need to purposely think God's thoughts. If you will memorize Scriptures and meditate on them day and night, it will change your life. It's difficult to speak or think negative things while you're dwelling on God's Word. It's almost impossible to be fearful or worried while God's promises are on your lips and in your thoughts. Before too long these truths will take root in your heart, and then you will become a doer of the Word, which is what God was telling Joshua here.

The Bible says that it's God's Word that increases our faith. (Rom. 10:17; Acts 20:32.) It also tells us that the Word is "the sword of the Spirit," the only offensive weapon in our God-given armor (Eph. 6:17). And Hebrews 4:12 says, "The word of God is full of living power. It is sharper than the sharpest knife." Meditating on God's Word makes tremendous power available to the believer. Jesus used it to defeat Satan when the devil came to tempt Him in the desert. We can use Scripture to overcome Satan's power, too. The next time the enemy tries to convince you that you're stupid or forgetful, you can tell him, "I have the mind of Christ!" (1 Cor. 2:16). If he comes against you with fear and worry, you can say, "God has not given me a spirit of fear, but of power, love, and a sound mind!" (2 Tim. 1:7). When the devil tries to convince you that you'll never overcome that sin you're struggling with, you can declare, "I've been set free from sin and I've become a slave to righteousness!" (Rom. 6:18). And when he tries to make you feel like you can't do anything right, you can tell him, "I can do all things through Christ who strengthens me!" (Phil. 4:13 NKJV). I challenge you today to take God's advice and begin thinking and speaking His Word day and night. If you do, the Lord's promise to you is that, "Then you will be prosperous and successful"!

LIVE ON PURPOSE TODAY

Search God's Word today for Scriptures that provide answers and change where you need it most. Commit to those Scriptures, memorize them, speak them over and over aloud to yourself, and then determine to live by them!

PRAYER

Lord, I thank You for Your Word. I ask that You help me to meditate on it and speak it day and night, so that I can overcome the power of the enemy. Plant it deep in my heart, Lord. Thank You that Your Word will make me prosperous and successful wherever I go!

He Sees Every Tear

*You keep track of all my sorrows. You have collected all my
tears in Your bottle. You have recorded each one in Your book.*

PSALM 56:8 NLT

Through these precious verses penned by David, God reveals
that He cares so deeply for us that He sees every tear and
preserves each one. Imagine the God of the universe tenderly preserving all our tears! The next time you feel alone and
forgotten, remember these verses and take heart. Rest assured
that ours is not a distant God, but one who is near to us, especially when we need Him most. Psalm 34:18 TLB says, "The Lord
is close to those whose hearts are breaking." The Bible is full of
Scriptures revealing God's love and compassion for us. In Isaiah
49:15-16 NLT, the Lord says, "Can a mother forget her nursing
child? Can she feel no love for a child she has borne? But even if
that were possible, I would not forget you! See, I have written
your name on My hand." Here again, God is assuring us that He is
not a distant, indifferent God, but a caring, intimate one. In Psalm
27:10 NLT, David writes, "Even if my father and mother abandon
me, the Lord will hold me close." If the whole world should
forsake us, God will never leave us. He is always only a prayer
away, and He will grant us His discernible presence when we ask
Him to.

Throughout the pages of the Bible, God reveals both His
might and His tenderness. Isaiah writes, "Who else has held the
oceans in His hand? Who has measured off the heavens with His

LIVE ON PURPOSE TODAY

There's no time like the present in which to enjoy God's discernible presence. Enter His gates with thanksgiving, enter His courts with praise, and experience His tender love and compassion.

fingers? Who else knows the weight of the earth or has weighed out the mountains and the hills?" (Isa. 40:12 NLT). Yet in the same passage, we find these verses: "He will feed His flock like a shepherd. He will carry the lambs in His arms, holding them close to His heart" (Isa. 40:11 NLT). And in Isaiah 66:13, the Lord says, "As a mother comforts her child, so will I comfort you." God's might is greater than anything we could imagine, and so is His tenderness. Rest assured that no problem is too big for Him to handle, and no pain is beyond His healing touch. If you are feeling alone, sad, or wounded today, it's my prayer that you will reach out in faith to our loving Lord and experience for yourself His comforting presence. The Savior's promise to you today is this: "I will not abandon you or leave you as orphans in the storm—I will come to you"! (John 14:18 TLB).

PRAYER

Lord, in times of despair and loneliness, I ask that You reveal to me Your tenderness and concern. Let me feel Your presence and reassure me that You are always near. Give me an understanding of Your indescribable love and compassion. Thank You that Your presence brings me comfort, healing, and joy!

Getting Serious About God's Promises

> *God is not a man, that he should lie. He is not a human, that he should change his mind. Has he ever spoken and failed to act? Has he ever promised and not carried it through?*
>
> NUMBERS 23:19 NLT

I've read many times that the Bible contains over 7,000 promises from God. Why did God go to such great lengths to record so many promises to His people? I must confess that it disturbs me sometimes that so many Christians have a "ho-hum" attitude toward God's promises. Next time you go to a Christian book store, notice how many "Promise" books there are. Why is that? Because a growing number of believers have discovered that praying and standing on God's promises can work miracles. I mean that literally. God's promises can give us hope in hopeless situations. Psalm 119:49-51 NLT says, "Remember your promise to me, for it is my only hope. Your promise revives me; it comforts me in all my troubles." If you are going through a trial, meditating on faith-building promises can give you the strength and hope you need to keep going when you would otherwise quit and give up. Also, try praying promise-centered prayers instead of problem-centered prayers, and I guarantee it will change your prayer life.

This doesn't mean that you can always pray a promise once or twice and have it come to pass. That does happen sometimes, of course, depending on the situation. But most of the time, we

LIVE ON PURPOSE TODAY

Get serious today about taking God at His Word by searching the Bible for Scriptures that build faith in you where you need it most!

have to go through a period of "standing" on a promise before the answer comes. Isaiah 62:6-7 NLT says, "...I have posted watchmen on your walls; they will pray to the Lord day and night for the fulfillment of his promises. Take no rest, all of you who pray. Give the Lord no rest...." The principle God is revealing to us here is that sometimes we have to persist in praying God's promises before they are fulfilled. Many times we give up praying before we receive an answer. Luke 18:1 TLB says, "One day Jesus told his disciples a story to illustrate their need for constant prayer and to show them that they must keep praying until the answer comes." Remember that "delays are not necessarily denials." The Bible teaches us that Jesus "carries out and fulfills all of God's promises, no matter how many of them there are" (2 Cor. 1:20 TLB). God is serious about His promises, and He honors those who take them seriously. But don't just take my word for it. Start getting serious about taking God at His Word, and discover for yourself that "He is the God who keeps every promise"! (Ps. 146:6 TLB).

PRAYER

Lord, I thank You for all Your "great and precious promises." Give me a new awareness of the purpose of Your promises, and a growing appreciation for them. Teach me how to meditate on faith-building promises, as well as how to pray promise-centered prayers. Thank You, Lord, that You are "faithful to all Your promises"! (Ps. 145:13).

Leading Others to the Lord

Don't have anything to do with foolish and stupid arguments, because you know they produce quarrels. And the Lord's servant must not quarrel; instead, he must be kind to everyone, able to teach, not resentful. Those who oppose him he must gently instruct, in the hope that God will grant them repentance leading them to a knowledge of the truth, and that they will come to their senses and escape from the trap of the devil, who has taken them captive to do his will.

2 TIMOTHY 2:23-26

I know what it's like to try to argue someone into the kingdom of God. I also know how futile it is to try to win people to Christ that way. I used to think that we should be able to convince people to believe the truth simply because it's the truth. But it doesn't work that way. Maybe that's not such a bad thing, though. Ron Luce of "Teen Mania" says, "If you can talk someone into Christianity, they can be talked out." Now I'm convinced that trying to argue someone into the kingdom can do more harm than good. In fact, the Bible warns against "quarreling about words" and says that not only is it "of no value," but it "only ruins those who listen" (2 Tim. 2:14). The verses above tell us that instead of arguing or debating with the unsaved, we should "gently instruct them." As the Holy Spirit leads us, we can attempt to teach those who don't believe by "speaking the truth in love," as Ephesians 4:15 says. Scripture goes on to say that we should do this in the hope that God will grant them repentance and lead them to a knowledge of the truth. Notice that it's God's part to grant them repentance and to lead them to the truth, not ours. That should take some of the pressure off of us. Sometimes we need to remind ourselves that we are not responsible for how others respond to the Gospel message. We're only responsible for how we deliver it.

Besides instructing the lost as we're led by God's Spirit, the verses above tell us that we must demonstrate godly character, being "kind to everyone, not resentful." Some people will not be reached when we tell them about Jesus, but they may be convinced if we *show* them Jesus. The apostle Paul confirms this when he writes, "Watch your life and your doctrine closely. Persevere in them, because if you do, you will save both yourself and your hearers" (1 Tim. 4:15,16). One evening several years ago I got a call from my teenage son saying that he had been in a car accident. He was unharmed, but his car was destroyed. I had visitors at the time, and one of them was an unsaved teen who no one had been able to reach with the Gospel. I found out later that as a result of my Christlike response to my son's accident, this girl gave her life to Christ. Since then, I've often wondered, *What if I had reacted differently?* It's so important for us to exhibit the fruit of the Spirit all the time. Lastly, there are times when all we can do for someone is pray for them. We may be the last ones they'll receive the truth from, and we may have to ask the Lord to put laborers in their path who they'll be receptive to. God

LIVE ON PURPOSE TODAY

Ask the Holy Spirit to bring across your heart the name of someone ripe for salvation today. Pray for that one, and also ask the Lord what role you are to play in the individual receiving Jesus Christ.

knows who they are. It's always wise for us to consult God and ask Him what our part is in leading someone to Him. My prayer for you today is that the Lord will use you in awesome ways to lead others to His kingdom!

PRAYER

Lord, open up doors of opportunity for me to lead others to You. Show me what my part is each time, and help me to be led by Your Spirit. Teach me to speak the truth in love and to set a Christlike example for others. Thank You for using me to touch and change lives for all eternity for Your glory!

Our Healing God

In those days Hezekiah became ill and was at the point of death. The prophet Isaiah son of Amoz went to him and said, "This is what the Lord says: Put your house in order, because you are going to die; you will not recover." Hezekiah turned his face to the wall and prayed to the Lord, "Remember, O Lord, how I have walked before you faithfully and with wholehearted devotion and have done what is good in your eyes." And Hezekiah wept bitterly. Then the word of the Lord came to Isaiah: "Go and tell Hezekiah, 'This is what the Lord, the God of your father David, says: I have heard your prayer and seen your tears; I will add fifteen years to your life.'" Isaiah had said, "Prepare a poultice of figs and apply it to the boil, and he will recover."

ISAIAH 38:1-5,21

In the above passage, though King Hezekiah was on his deathbed and had already been told by the prophet Isaiah that he would not recover, he pleads with the Lord to deliver him. Many of us would have just accepted the bad report we had received; yet this man of faith sought God's mercy and power in his darkest hour. God not only healed him, but He increased his life another fifteen years as well. I believe that God is using Hezekiah as an example here to show us how essential prayer is when we are in need of healing. I also believe the Lord is illustrating how He sometimes uses practical remedies in the healing process. Notice that the prophet Isaiah prescribed a fig poultice for the king, no doubt at God's direction. God did the healing, but He used a simple treatment to bring about recovery. I believe that

God can anoint an herb, vitamin, or medicine to promote healing. And He can use doctors to prescribe beneficial remedies, just as He used Isaiah here.

Second Chronicles 16:12-13 records that King Asa "was afflicted with a disease in his feet. Though his disease was severe, even in his illness he did not seek help from the Lord, but only from the physicians." The next verse reveals that Asa died from this affliction. This is a very clear warning to all of us. If we choose to depend on doctors and remedies apart from seeking God, we could be risking our health, or even our lives. Another lesson Scripture teaches us about healing is that it can be a gradual process. In Mark 8:22-26, Jesus lays hands on a blind man twice before his sight is completely restored. While I do believe in instantaneous healings, I believe that most healings take time. And just like Jesus used various methods to heal, God may use one way to heal you, and another to heal someone else, even though you both have the same ailment. The next time you're ill, turn to God first for help. Ask Him for His wisdom, according to His promise in James 1:5. Search out God's many promises of healing in the Scriptures—pray and stand on them. My prayer is that when you do, you'll soon be able to declare, "O Lord my God, I called to you for help and you healed me"! (Ps. 30:2).

LIVE ON PURPOSE TODAY

Take this opportunity to read aloud to yourself God's promises of healing. Faith will rise in your heart, and God's Word will be medicine to all your flesh.

PRAYER

*Lord, when illness threatens, send Your Word and heal me.
(Ps. 107:20.) Show me when I should see a doctor and who it
should be, and give them Your wisdom and skill. Spare me
from all unnecessary and unpleasant tests and treatments.
Reveal to me what supplements or medicines would help, and anoint
them for my use. Teach me how to walk in health and wholeness.
Thank You that You have promised to be my Healer! (Ex. 15:26.)*

Turning Misery Into Ministry

*It was a beautiful thing that you came
alongside me in my troubles.*

PHILIPPIANS 4:14 MESSAGE

I recently had my first root canal. I was having some persistent problems with my teeth, and as the possibility of having to have a root canal loomed larger, I earnestly prayed that the Lord would spare me from it. As it turned out, this dental procedure that I had always dreaded was my only recourse, and I couldn't avoid it any longer. I prayed through the entire thing, and I trusted the Lord to walk me through it. When it was over, I was brooding about having to go through this unpleasant experience, and I sensed the Lord reassuring me that it was not in vain—that He would bring much good out of it. A week or so later I was at a family gathering, and I found myself exclaiming to one of my relatives, "I had my first root canal!" I realized that I was taking some perverse pleasure in experiencing this unpleasant procedure first-hand, and initially, I was baffled by my attitude. Then it hit me. I was feeling a tremendous sense of satisfaction and joy in being able to say to others who have had root canals—"I understand how you feel. I've been there, and I know what you're going through."

One thing is clear—it's scriptural to pray for protection and deliverance from trouble. But I do think that there are times when God allows us to experience adversity firsthand so that we can develop a heart of compassion toward others who are suffering. I know that this has been true in my own life, and I have seen trials soften the hearts of others, too. I certainly don't recommend praying for trouble. But I also don't recommend succumbing to despair or doubt when adversity is staring us in the face. God is a mighty and compassionate God, and He can—and will—bring good out of even the most daunting circumstances, if we will firmly place our trust in Him and maintain a right attitude during these times. Having to go through painful and difficult experiences can also help us to pray more effectively for others who are in trouble. When I hear from parents who are dealing with harrowing problems with their children, it's easy for me to feel their anguish because of my own painful experiences as a parent. I believe that my prayers for these parents are much more fervent and effective since I've developed a greater understanding and empathy toward their plight.

LIVE ON PURPOSE TODAY

Practice what's been preached to you and ask the Lord to help you see your problems from a heavenly perspective. He'll turn your misery into ministry!

David wrote, "I will be glad and rejoice in your love, for you saw my affliction and knew the anguish of my soul" (Ps. 31:7). Though these words refer to the Lord, they can also apply to those of us who have become more Christlike through our trials and tribulations. We, too, can have a greater depth of love and compassion toward others. We can relate to their suffering and feel their pain. And we can be a great source of comfort and joy to them. Today, I encourage you to ask the Lord to help you see your problems from a heavenly perspective. Pray that God will enable you to believe that He can turn your misery into ministry. Then you will know firsthand the joy and satisfaction of being able to say with all sincerity—"I understand what you're going through, and I'm praying for you!"

PRAYER

Lord, teach me how to pray in faith for protection and deliverance from trouble. When I do experience tests and trials, help me to understand their value. Give me the faith I need to believe that You will bring good out of every adversity I face. (Rom. 8:28.) Thank You that by Your grace my difficulties will make me a more compassionate person and a more effective intercessor!

For Heaven's Sake, ASK!

You do not have, because you do not ask God.

JAMES 4:2

Almost every Christian who knows anything about the Bible knows Psalm 37:4, which says, "Delight yourself in the Lord, and he will give you the desires of your heart." But the verse from James quoted above is a lot less familiar. The Bible contains countless verses which promise God's people the desires of their hearts, or which encourage us to "ask." If you ever entertain the idea that our God doesn't care about your heart's desires, just pick up any little book of God's promises and look up "joy" or "prayer." I guarantee it will change your mind. One of my favorites is in John 16:24, where Jesus says, "Ask and you will receive, and your joy will be complete" (John 16:24).

I often hear people say things like, "I wish I had a different job," or "I wish I had a new car." Or even, "I wish I were doing better in school," or "I wish my spouse would be more considerate." Many times, I'm tempted to ask, "Did you pray about it? Did you know that we serve a God who wants to meet all your needs and even give you the desires of your heart, if you'll only ask Him? "I'm inclined to agree with those who say that Christians should have a little less "wishbone" and a little more backbone. While it's true that we are not always wise enough to ask for what's good for us, let's not forget that we are invited to ask. I have found that I usually feel most comfortable asking God for my heart's desire, and then telling Him, "But Lord, most of all—I pray Thy will be done."

That way I know I'll get God's best. Could it be that the only reason you lack certain blessings right now is because you haven't asked God for them? Absolutely! Today, start taking God up on His generous offer by asking Him for the desires of your heart, and then prepare to be bombarded with blessings!

LIVE ON PURPOSE TODAY

Spend some time drawing your desires out of your heart, and then take God up on His offer. Ask Him in faith for your desires, and then let the bombardment begin.

PRAYER

Lord, I thank You that You love me so much that, not only do You want to meet my needs, but You want to give me my heart's desires as well. I ask that You give me a new heart today so that the desires of my heart will never conflict with the desires of Yours. Help me to see that if the answer to my prayer will glorify You, it may not only be my privilege to ask, but my obligation. Thank You for Your promise which says that You will "satisfy my desires with good things so that my youth is renewed like the eagle's!"

Quietly Trusting the Lord

"Lord, my heart is not proud; my eyes are not haughty. I don't concern myself with matters too great or awesome for me. But I have stilled and quieted myself, just as a small child is quiet with its mother. Yes, like a small child is my soul within me. O Israel, put your hope in the Lord—now and always."

PSALM 131:1-3 NLT

I f you've ever been closely involved with making plans for a wedding in one respect or another, like I have, you know how stressful it can be. My son John's wedding this past summer was no exception. At one point, when we were faced with making seating arrangements for the wedding reception, I began feeling completely overwhelmed. As I turned to the Lord in prayer, asking Him for an extra measure of His wisdom and strength, He led me to Psalm 131.

Here, David says, "Lord, my heart is not proud; my eyes are not haughty. I don't concern myself with matters too great or awesome for me" (v. 1). Reading these words enabled me to breathe a sigh of relief. Suddenly, I realized that not only did God not *expect* me to handle matters by myself, but He didn't even *want* me trying to handle them on my own. In fact, in God's eyes, if I tried to deal with my concerns without relying on Him for help, I would be seen as "proud" and "haughty"—two characteristics that the Bible says are detestable in His sight.

David goes on to say, "But I have stilled and quieted myself, just as a small child is quiet with its mother. Yes, like a small child is my soul within me" (v. 2). I realized then that the Lord wanted me to calm and quiet myself before Him, just like a child resting in the arms of a loving parent would. Instead, I had been fretting about my concerns and talking about them constantly, rather than praying about them and laying them at the Lord's feet, like He wanted me to. Jesus said, "I tell you the truth, unless you *change* and become like little children, you will never enter the kingdom of heaven" (Matt 18:3). Receiving God's precious gift of salvation requires us to humble ourselves before God, in childlike faith. The same is true when it comes to receiving many of the other blessings the Lord desires to bestow on us, both spiritual and earthly. Psalm 46:10 says, "Be still, and know that I am God." The New American Standard translation puts it this way: "*Cease striving* and know that I am God." There are times when all of us need to hear this

LIVE ON PURPOSE TODAY

Take a few minutes today to just sit quietly and listen to what God is speaking to your heart.

reminder—that if we will settle down and let God be God of our lives and circumstances, He will take control of everything that seems out of control, and He will turn our messes into miracles.

David beautifully concludes Psalm 131 with the statement, "You too should *quietly trust* in the Lord—now and always" (v. 3 TLB). When we're in the midst of troubling circumstances—when the enemy's voice is whispering in our ears, "What are you going to do?"—we can turn to the King of Kings and Lord of Lords and say—"We do not know what to do, but our eyes are upon You"! (2 Chron. 20:12).

PRAYER

Lord, when I'm facing situations that have me feeling overwhelmed, confused, or frightened, remind me that I don't have to concern myself with matters that are "too great or awesome for me." Teach me how to "still and quiet myself" before You in childlike faith and to entrust to You all that concerns me. Thank You that as I "quietly trust" in You, I will come out on top in every situation and circumstance!

What Happens When We Share With the God of Increase

Another of his disciples, Andrew, Simon Peter's brother, spoke up, "Here is a boy with five small barley loaves and two small fish, but how far will they go among so many?"

JOHN 6:9

It has always amazed me to read about this boy who offered up his bread and fish for the multitude. What was he thinking? Didn't he realize how inadequate such a meager portion would be among so many? And could he have been the only one out of all those thousands of people who had any food with him that day? Not likely. The rest were either reluctant to share what they had, or they figured that what they had to offer would be nothing more than a worthless contribution. The Scriptures tell us that just this one boy offered up his meal to the Lord. As a result, one of the greatest miracles recorded in the Gospels comes to pass.

Have you ever felt that you didn't have much to offer anyone, let alone God? If He can feed a multitude with just a few loaves and fishes, imagine what He could do with even your most meager resources. Try offering God your time, material resources, and talents, and give Him the opportunity to use you in ways you could never imagine!

PRAYER

LIVE ON PURPOSE TODAY

Report to God for duty today! Offer Him the time you have available—or time you will make available—and watch Him multiply what can be accomplished for His kingdom.

Lord, forgive me for the times I've failed to share my personal resources with You and others, especially when there are so many people in need. Help me to see all the potential good that even the smallest gifts You've given me can do. Give me the faith and compassion to wholeheartedly offer them up to You so that others may be blessed and You may be glorified.

Judge Not

Don't pick on people, jump on their failures, criticize their faults—unless, of course, you want the same treatment. Don't condemn those who are down; that hardness can boomerang. Be easy on people; you'll find life a lot easier.

LUKE 6:37 MESSAGE

T he New King James Version of this verse reads, "Judge not, and you shall not be judged...." But I like The Message Bible version best because it graphically depicts how destructive our judgment of others can be—and how it can come back to haunt us. Jesus warns us here that whenever we sow seeds of condemnation and criticism, we can count on reaping the same kind of harvest for ourselves. Next time someone criticizes you, ask yourself if you are truly a victim of injustice, or if you're just reaping the consequences of criticizing others. Pray and ask the Lord which case applies to you, and be quick to repent of any wrongdoing. Then ask God to comfort you and help you be less judgmental in the future. I've heard it said that we judge others by their actions, and ourselves by our good intentions. Perhaps that's because we have an idea what's in our own hearts, but we can't see into the hearts of others. The Bible says, "The Lord does not look at the things man looks at. Man looks at the outward appearance, but the Lord looks at the heart" (1 Sam. 16:7). Because only God can see into a person's heart, He doesn't want us judging our neighbors. Jesus said, "Stop judging by mere appearances, and make a right judgment." Yes, it's true that we need to be discerning, especially when choosing our closest companions, but judgment is an entirely different matter, and the Bible gives numerous warnings against it.

James 4:12 says, "There is only one Lawgiver and Judge, the one who is able to save and destroy. But you—who are you to judge your neighbor?" When God judges people, it's because He has the right to judge us, and because He is a righteous Judge. But when we judge others, usually pride is at the root of our judgment. Most of the time we are doing it with an attitude that lifts ourselves up, while putting others down. In 1 Corinthians 4:5, Paul writes, "Judge nothing before the appointed time; wait till the Lord comes. He will bring to light what is hidden in darkness and will expose the motives of men's hearts." And in Romans 14:13, he says, "Each of us will give an account of himself to God. Therefore, let us stop passing judgment on one another." Paul warns us to shift our focus from others to ourselves. In 1 Corinthians 11:31, he urges us to "judge ourselves." And in Galatians 6:4, he says, "Each one should test his own actions." I have found that the more time I spend examining my own conduct, the less inclined I am to focus on the behavior of others. Some of the best advice I've ever gotten from the Scriptures is in 1 Thessalonians 4:11. It says, "Mind your own business." I find that I have much more peace and joy in my life when I just stay out of other people's business. Yes, there are times we need to confront others about their behavior, and the Bible addresses that issue. "If

LIVE ON PURPOSE TODAY

Devote a few moments to examining your behavior and conduct. Such self-introspection will make you less inclined to judge others.

someone is caught in a sin, you who are spiritual should restore him gently. But watch yourself, or you also may be tempted" (Gal. 6:1). If we feel that God is directing us to confront someone, we must do it with gentleness and humility, resisting the temptation to be prideful. The intent here should be restoration, rather than condemnation. Scripture says, "I desire mercy, not sacrifice" (Matt. 9:13). God is not impressed with our good deeds or service when our hearts are filled with judgment for our neighbor. Jesus said, "Blessed are the merciful, for they will be shown mercy" (Matt. 5:7). May we all begin today to sow seeds of mercy, that we may reap a bountiful harvest of mercy from our gracious God.

PRAYER

Lord, teach me to spend more time showing others mercy, and less time judging them. Help me to be led by Your Spirit when I need to confront someone about their behavior. Show me how to examine my own actions and to be quick to repent of any wrongdoing. Thank You that my heart of mercy will draw others to You!

Praying for Ourselves

Jabez cried out to the God of Israel, "Oh, that you would bless me and enlarge my territory! Let your hand be with me, and keep me from harm so that I will be free from pain." And God granted his request.

1 CHRONICLES 4:10

I often hear from Christians who confess that they are feeling depressed, defeated, and weary. Many of them tell me that they do a lot of praying for others, but very little for themselves. Over the years I've begun to see a distinct pattern here. For some reason these people believe it's right and noble to pray for others but not for themselves. They often have no trouble asking God to pour out His blessings upon someone else, but they falter when they consider praying the same things for their own lives. As a result, they often wrestle with feelings of doubt, insecurity, and weakness. If you are one of these people, my heart goes out to you. I understand your struggles because I have experienced them myself.

Let me assure you today that it is very scriptural for believers to pray for themselves. The Bible is filled with examples of God's people praying for themselves and receiving extraordinary blessings as a result. I'm thankful that Jabez's prayer, as recorded in 1 Chronicles 4:10, has recently become very popular. Through this simple but powerful prayer, Christians are gaining a new awareness of just how important it is for them to pray for themselves. Jabez pleads, "Oh, that You would bless me and enlarge my territory! Let Your hand be with me, and keep me from harm so that I will be free from pain." I especially like the Living Bible translation which says, "Oh, that You would wonderfully bless me!" If God's people would pray for themselves with such abandon, there's no telling what the body of Christ could accomplish for His glory. We know that the Lord was pleased with Jabez's prayer, because the last line in the verse states, "And God granted his request." (Hallelujah!)

I thank the Lord that He gave us examples in the Bible of Jesus, Paul, David, and others praying for themselves. (See John 17:1-5, 2 Corinthians 12:8, and Psalm 4:1.) David, in particular, gave us a wealth of prayers he prayed for himself, as recorded in Psalms. We know that he was "a man after God's own heart" (Acts 13:22) and that he lived a life of unparalleled victory. David left us Spirit-led prayers we could pray for ourselves so that we, too, could walk in victory and become all God created us to be. In Psalm 143:10, he wrote, "Teach me to do Your will, for You are my God; may Your good Spirit lead me on level ground." I believe that one reason why David was so dear to the Lord, and so blessed, was because he constantly asked God for guidance, strength, joy, peace, prosperity, deliverance, and other blessings. The Scriptures make it abundantly clear that David didn't hesitate to pray for himself, so why should we?

LIVE ON PURPOSE TODAY

Today, you must pray for yourself! Share with the Lord your goals, dreams, needs, and deficiencies. And then ask for His abundant supply and provision in every area.

The fact that many people feel weak when they neglect to pray for themselves is no coincidence. Praying for ourselves invites the blessings of God into our lives and makes us strong in spirit. It also makes us less vulnerable to satanic attack. The last thing Satan wants us to do is pray for God to strengthen us, to help us do His will, and to equip us for victory. That's one reason why he'll often try to attack us with feelings of guilt and condemnation when we pray for ourselves. Jesus told His disciples, "Pray that you will not fall into temptation" (Luke 22:40). The same devil that came against the disciples during Jesus' day is the same devil that will come against us today. And praying for God's help is just as important now as it was back then. Personally, I spend a lot of time each day praying for others. Sometimes I become so preoccupied with lifting others up to the Lord that I neglect to pray for myself. When this happens, it isn't long before I notice myself becoming weak and weary. That's when I remind myself that if I don't spend a certain amount of time praying for my own needs, I won't be much good to anyone else. Let me encourage you today to keep yourself in prayer. Keep asking the Lord to bless you abundantly so that you can be a blessing to others and give Him all the glory He deserves!

PRAYER

Lord, I confess that there are times when I feel less than enthusiastic about praying for myself. Please change my heart, and help me to realize that it really is Your will for me. Teach me how to pray for my own needs—even when those needs include peace, joy, strength, and faith. Thank You that as I stay strong in spirit, You will use me in greater ways for Your glory!

The Appearance of Evil

Abstain from all appearance of evil.

1 THESSALONIANS 5:22 KJV

Some months ago I heard from a young teen who asked for prayer because she was having a hard time finding a job. She described herself as looking like a "punk druggie," but assured me that she was "straight-edge" and a "strong Christian." She was frustrated because everyone, including potential employers, seemed focused on her appearance, whereas she desperately wanted them to focus on her "personality" and "maturity." What she didn't understand was the fact that, in many cases, all she had to do was to *look* like a rebellious, drug-using teen to be mistaken for one.

The Bible says, "Abstain from all appearance of evil" (1 Thess. 5:22 KJV). No matter how good this teen's intentions might be, and no matter how much she might love the Lord, He *is* concerned about her appearance and about the kind of impression she makes on those she comes in contact with. Scripture says that God is the only One who can see into people's hearts (1 Kings 8:39), and because of that, the believer's outward appearance, actions, and words must be consistently Christlike, if we're to make a real difference for Him in this world. The Amplified Version of this verse reads, "Abstain from evil [shrink from it and keep aloof from it] in whatever form or whatever kind it may be." If we are to please and glorify God, we must keep a healthy distance from "every kind of evil."

Avoiding even the "appearance" of evil or wrongdoing can apply to our relationships, too. A Christian wife or husband should think twice before they spend time alone with someone of the opposite sex. They may be tempted to think, *But I'm not doing anything wrong, and God knows that.* Even if this is true and our intentions are good, it's our duty as servants of Christ to consider how our conduct might appear to those around us. The Bible says, "Take thought for what is honest and proper and noble [aiming to be above reproach] in the sight of everyone" (Rom. 12:17 AMP). If our actions could be construed by others as being improper or less than noble, then chances are that we are not being Spirit-led and we are catering to our own emotions and desires. Instead, God wants us to, "Be careful to do what is right in the eyes of everybody" (Rom. 12:17).

This teen who wrote me desperately wanted to be seen as a mature individual. But the Bible indicates that there's a price that needs to be paid for this kind of privilege. First Timothy 4:12 says, "Don't let anyone look down on you because you are young, but set an example for the believers in speech, in life, in love, in faith and in purity." Because this girl was not setting a Christlike example to others, she was allowing others to look down on her and to see her in a less-than-positive light.

LIVE ON PURPOSE TODAY

Take a trip to the mirror today and take a good long look at yourself. Does your image avoid any appearance of evil and appropriately represent Jesus Christ? Do you also avoid the appearance of evil in your relationships and associations? Determine to radiate heavenly citizenship everywhere you go.

Christians can't afford to have an attitude that says—"I don't care what anyone thinks. I'm going to do what I want and look the way I want!" We are not just responsible to ourselves, but we are first and foremost responsible to our God. And if we will make it our goal to honor Him with every aspect of our lives, He will bless us, promote us, and use us to make an eternal difference in this world!

PRAYER

Lord, teach me how to avoid even the appearance of evil in every area of my life. Guard me from having a too carefree or careless attitude about my appearance, my relationships, or my conduct.
Thank You that as I strive to set a Christlike example in everything, You will use me to change the world around me!

Our Rightful Source

This is what the Lord says: "Cursed is the one who trusts in man, who depends on flesh for his strength and whose heart turns away from the Lord....
But blessed is the man who trusts in the Lord, whose confidence is in him. He will be like a tree planted by the water that sends out its roots by the stream...."

JEREMIAH 17:5,7,8

I like the way God doesn't mince words. He makes it abundantly clear that He wants us to put our trust in Him and not man. He goes so far as to say that those who put their trust in people will be cursed. Isaiah 2:22 says, "Stop trusting in man, who has but a breath in his nostrils. Of what account is he?" I especially like the way David puts it in Psalm 60:11: "Give us aid against the enemy, for the help of man is worthless." And for those of us who are tempted to put our trust in leaders, Psalm 146:3 says, "Do not put your trust in princes, in mortal men who cannot save." But the verses above reassure us that those who put their trust in God will not have to fear or worry even in a year of drought, because they will always be fresh and fruitful!

A job can be a good thing, but God doesn't want us making it our source. If we do, when we lose it, we will have no means of support. On the other hand, if we make God our provider, even if we are jobless for a time, our needs will still be met. Doctors can definitely be a blessing. But if we rely only on their limited wisdom and leave God out of the picture, it could cost us our health—

maybe even our lives. Spouses and parents can be wonderful gifts, but depending on them for all our needs can be disastrous if they're ever taken from us. The good news is that God is willing and able to be all that we need in this life. If you are looking for stability and security in this ever-changing world, make our unchangeable God the source of all your needs. Then you can exclaim with the psalmist, "O Lord Almighty, blessed is the man who trusts in you"! (Ps. 84:12).

LIVE ON PURPOSE

This would be a good opportunity to count your blessings literally one by one. What better way is there to properly recognize your source? As a testimony to God's goodness, begin to list on paper the ways He's blessed you the most, and then keep that list nearby to encourage yourself in times of trouble.

PRAYER

Lord, forgive me for the times I put my trust in man, rather than You. Help me to look to You for all my needs, including all my physical, emotional, and spiritual needs. Help me to realize that when I make You my source, my resources are boundless. Thank You that no matter what happens, I will always be blessed and fruitful!

The Price of Peace Is Prayer

Do not be anxious about anything, but in everything, by prayer and petition, with thanksgiving, present your requests to God. And the peace of God, which transcends all understanding, will guard your hearts and your minds in Christ Jesus.

PHILIPPIANS 4:6,7

These verses were the ones that convinced me that God really does want us to pray about everything. Here, Paul tells us that there is nothing in life that we should worry about. Then he says that, instead, we should pray about everything. When I first read these verses, I thought for sure there must be exceptions to the rule. Surely God has better things to do than to listen to my every little complaint or concern. Wrong. Look at it this way—whatever we don't pray about, we're going to worry about, right? And the point God is trying to make here is that He doesn't want us worrying about anything. That means that there's nothing that's too trivial to bring to God's attention in prayer.

Years ago I was told by well-meaning people that I was not to bother God with the little details of life. I have seen many precious people struggle with burdens that God is willing to lighten for them, all because they were under the impression that He's too busy or disinterested in their minor affairs. Now, when I tell you that I pray about everything, you can believe I mean everything. I don't wait until my little problems become big problems. I present them to God right away, and even when He doesn't answer my prayers the way I expect Him to, He always does something to ease the strain. Don't buy into that misconception that says God is not interested in every little detail of your life. Start today to pray about anything and everything that concerns you, and then enjoy the peace and satisfaction that settle over you when you do!

LIVE ON PURPOSE TODAY

What problems and frustrations did you carry yesterday that you could have turned over to the Lord? Make note of them so that today you can walk carefree!

PRAYER

Lord, I'm sorry for all the times I carried burdens I didn't have to, all because I neglected to bring them to You in prayer. Open my eyes and my heart, and help me to see how much You love me and how much You care about every little concern of mine. Whenever I am tempted to shoulder my burdens alone, please remind me to turn to You in prayer, and then surround me with Your perfect, healing peace.

Lunatic, Liar, or Lord?

{ *But what about you?" [Jesus] asked. "Who do you say I am?"*
MATTHEW 16:15 }

At a recent gathering, my family and I got into what I call a "lively discussion" about some of the literal meanings of the Bible. The subject of the parting of the Red Sea came up, and some family members tried to explain the "truth" behind the actual event. When one of my family members essentially asked me—"You don't *really* believe it happened the way it's written in the Bible, do you?"—the only answer I could give was that Jesus believed it, and that was good enough for me. Through careful and prayerful study of the Bible in recent years, I've realized that one thing is certain: Jesus believed the Scriptures were true. He even called them "the Word of God" (John 10:35). That leaves us with only three choices: Christ was (1) a lunatic, (2) a liar, or (3) He was exactly who He said He was—the Son of the living God. He states this clearly in John 10:36 when He says, "I am God's Son." Jesus also makes it clear that what we believe about Him will determine where we spend eternity. In John 8:24, He says, "If you do not believe that I am the One I claim to be, you will indeed die in your sins." Jesus believed in the infallibility of the Bible. He said, "I tell you the truth, until heaven and earth disappear, not the smallest letter, not the least stroke of a pen, will by any means disappear from the Law until everything is accomplished" (Matt. 5:18). He also said, "the Scripture cannot be broken" (John 10:35). Jesus called God's Word "Truth" (John 17:17). He even called Himself "the Truth" (John 14:6). He said that those who reject Him and don't accept His words as truth will be condemned. (John 12:48.) It's obvious that Jesus doesn't leave us any room to doubt the veracity of God's Word. Either we believe it—and Him—or we don't.

After a Christian concert I attended some years ago, the lead singer gave an inspiring talk, and he said something that was life-changing for me. He said that it didn't matter to him what discoveries science made because nothing could shake his faith. He knew his God and believed His Word. From that day on I made a quality decision not to put any stock in scientific discoveries that refuted, or even supported, God's Word. Every time I hear about strong scientific evidence supporting the Bible, I eventually hear evidence refuting it. God doesn't want us putting our faith in science, technology, or archeology. He wants us to put our faith solely in Him and His Word. Jesus said that only those with child-like faith would enter the kingdom of God. That's because we're going to have to deal with a lot of unanswered questions and still trust God while we're in this world. Those who try to figure out God, or who try to find scientific or logical explanations for His actions, will

LIVE ON PURPOSE TODAY

Seek God in prayer and praise today and devote extra time to Bible reading. Focus on Scriptures that answer who Jesus really is.

not be entrusted with an intimate knowledge of His awesome character and truth. Jesus said, "I praise you, O Father, Lord of heaven and earth, for hiding these things from the intellectuals and worldly wise and for revealing them to those who are as trusting as little children. Yes, thank you, Father, for that is the way you wanted it" (Luke 10:21,22 TLB). If you tried to convince me that the God of the Bible isn't real, or that His Word isn't true, I'd have to tell you that you're too late. As the apostle Paul said, "I know whom I have believed" (2 Tim. 1:12). To me, Jesus is not a lunatic or a liar. He's my Lord. I've given Him His rightful place in my life, and because of that, He's revealed Himself to me in awesome ways. Because I believe His promises and take them personally, I see them come to pass in my life. Those who doubt the truth of God's Word and His promises will never profit from them. (Heb. 4:2.) If you believe the way I do, don't ever let anyone ruin your faith or cause you to doubt. Paul wrote, "Don't let others spoil your faith and joy with their philosophies, their wrong and shallow answers built on men's thoughts and ideas, instead of on what Christ has said" (Col. 2:8 TLB). Faith is not a feeling; it's a decision. The Bible says that God has given every man a measure of faith. (Rom. 12:3.) That means that all of us have the ability to believe God. But we have to choose to believe. When we do, God has promised to reveal Himself to us. (John 11:40.) Jesus asked His disciples, "Who do you say I am?" Today, He's asking you the same thing. How will you answer Him?

PRAYER

Lord, please give me the faith I need to believe Your Word and act on it for Your glory. Help me to do my part by seeking You daily in prayer, praise, and Bible reading. I pray that my faith would become so unshakable that nothing anyone says or does can spoil it. I surrender my all to You, Jesus, and I thank You for being my Lord!

The Recipe for Success

Commit everything you do to the Lord.
Trust him, and he will help you.

PSALM 37:5 NLT

The Bible contains many promises related to the tasks we perform. The verse above is one of my favorites to pray and stand on whenever I have a job to do. Another one is Proverbs 16:3, "Commit your work to the Lord, and then your plans will succeed." God is eager to bless the work of our hands, and He wants us to succeed in all we do. Notice, though, that He wants us to first entrust our tasks to Him. God wants to be invited into every area of our daily lives, but He is a gentleman. He will not force His help on us. That's not His style. There's a certain amount of humility involved in our asking God for help, and often it's our pride that keeps us from asking. Other times it's the belief that it's not a big enough job to seek God's help with, or it's one that we've performed countless times before. I'm familiar with that way of thinking because I used to think that way myself. Now, no matter how small or insignificant my tasks seem, I ask God for His help, and I believe it pleases Him greatly. How do I know? Because overall, my work goes more smoothly, the results are better, and I experience more joy and satisfaction.

Next time you start to fix your hair or apply your makeup, ask for the Lord's help. When you're doing the laundry, mowing the lawn, or working on your car, invite God to help you. Commit all your child care and parenting duties to Him. Don't try to raise

LIVE ON PURPOSE TODAY

Purpose to seek God's help in every activity of the day. What one thing immediately comes to mind that you can commit to the Lord right now? As soon as you commit to Him, you've already begun following God's recipe for success!

kids these days without the divine assistance that God offers you. Don't try to drive without Him. Take the Lord along with you when you travel. And why would any child of God want to try to get through school without their heavenly Father's grace, power, and wisdom? If you're employed, bring God to your job each day, and ask Him to help you be the best employee your company's ever had. When you "commit everything you do to the Lord," you will have at your disposal the help of the Father, Son, and Holy Spirit, as well as a legion of angels, if necessary. Today, begin seeking God's help in all your endeavors, and you can bet "the Lord your God will make you successful in everything you do"! (Deut. 30:9 NLT).

PRAYER

Lord, I'm sorry that I've often left You out of my everyday activities. Help me to humble myself and ask You for help with everything I do. When I'm tempted to try to do things on my own, remind me of Your generous offer to help. Deliver me from an independent attitude, and help me to rely on You the way You desire. Thank You for the greater ease, joy, and success I'll find in all my tasks from now on!

When All We Can
See Are Giants!

> *The land we passed through and explored is exceedingly good.*
> *If the Lord is pleased with us, he will lead us into that land,*
> *a land flowing with milk and honey, and will give it to us. Only*
> *do not rebel against the Lord. And do not be afraid of the people*
> *of the land, because we will swallow them up. Their protection is*
> *gone, but the Lord is with us. Do not be afraid of them.*
>
> NUMBERS 14:7-9

These are the words of Joshua and Caleb after returning from their exploration of the Promised Land, along with ten other "spies" sent out by Moses, their leader. God had promised the land of Canaan to the Israelites after He delivered them out of the hands of Pharoah in Egypt. The Lord had told His people that the land He was giving them was lush and fertile—"a land flowing with milk and honey." When the twelve spies scouted out the land in advance, they discovered that "all the people there were of great size" (Num. 13:32), and as a result, ten of the spies brought back a "bad report." Only Joshua and Caleb declared that they were able to conquer the giants, because God was on their side. And because of their faith in God and His promises in the face of certain defeat, they were the only two spies that made it to the Promised Land.

You may have some giants looming in your life right now. They may be financial troubles or health problems, or problems

LIVE ON PURPOSE TODAY

To help magnify God in your life and minimize your problems, go to God's Word and find Scriptures that promise you victory over the giants you face. Memorize at least one of those Scriptures and quote it throughout the day!

with a parent, child, teacher, or boss. Maybe you've been struggling with your weight for years, and you don't see any way out. Whatever it is, remember Joshua and Caleb. When the other ten spies saw only giants, Joshua and Caleb saw God. There's a song that says, "Turn your eyes upon Jesus." If you'll do that today, God will see to it that you make it to the Promised Land!

PRAYER

Lord, You know what I'm up against today. Sometimes my problems seem so big that all I can see is them and not You. Help me to take my eyes off the giants in my life and fix them on You. Cause me to realize how big a God You really are and how willing You are to face all my problems with me, if I'll let You. Thank You that with You beside me, the victory is mine!

Putting Off Procrastination

{ *"If you wait for perfect conditions,*
you will never get anything done."

ECCLESIASTES 11:4 NLT }

The dictionary defines *procrastinate* as "to put off doing until a future time, especially to postpone habitually."[1] I used to think that procrastination was just a harmless, annoying habit, but I've discovered through studying the Scriptures that it can be a highly destructive way of life. In fact, Proverbs 18:9 says, "One who is slack in his work is brother to one who destroys." The above verse from Ecclesiastes warns us that if we wait for "perfect conditions" to perform our tasks, we'll never accomplish anything. Did you ever notice that when you keep putting off something you dread doing, it looms larger and larger in front of you? That's because when we procrastinate, we allow feelings of dread to control us. Over time the sense that we're losing control can grow increasingly stronger and overwhelm us. If we let it, procrastination can actually become a form of bondage and paralyze us. It can steal our joy and peace, and lead to anxiety and depression. It can rob us of our dignity and our self-esteem. When we put off a task or obligation, we don't improve our situation, and in fact, we usually make it worse. Procrastination never simplifies our lives, even though it may appear that way sometimes, but it actually complicates our lives and increases our stress levels. No matter what's at the root of our procrastination—fear, feelings of inadequacy, laziness—the fruit of it is always rotten.

When I'm faced with a task I'm really dreading, I try to focus on how good I'm going to feel after it's done, rather than on the task itself. Often that helps me get started, and getting started is usually the hardest part. That's why it's so important to ask the Lord to help us take that first step. If we remember that God has given us a spirit of discipline (2 Tim. 1:7) and that self-control is a fruit of the Spirit (Gal. 5:23), we'll be better equipped to resist the enemy's attempts to make us believe that we're incapable of following through. Proverbs 3:27-28 says, "Do not withhold good from those who deserve it, when it is in your power to act. Do not say to your neighbor, 'Come back later; I'll give it tomorrow'—when you now have it with you." God doesn't want us putting off doing good to others. When His Spirit prompts us to call someone, send them a card, or visit them, we need to be quick to respond. Our timely response can make a world of difference in someone else's life. While procrastination robs us of blessings, God promises us great rewards for practicing diligence. The Bible says that diligent hands "bring wealth" and "will rule" (Prov. 10:4; 12:24). And Proverbs 13:4 says, "The desires of the diligent are fully satisfied." Often when we pray and ask the Lord for the desires of our hearts, He will expect us to play a part in the process. Whether the work involved is challenging and exciting, or mundane and monotonous, if we approach our tasks with a conscientious attitude, we will find great reward and satisfaction as a

LIVE ON PURPOSE TODAY

Is there a task you've been dreading and putting off? Delay no longer. This is the moment to begin! One small step and the hardest part will be over.

result. Proverbs 12:27 says, "The diligent man prizes his possessions." When we put care and effort into maintaining the things God has blessed us with—our homes, cars, etc.—we show God and others that we are truly thankful for them. It's this kind of attitude that delights the heart of God and opens the door to even greater rewards. From now on, think of procrastinating as putting off your blessings, and resist it with the Holy Spirit power that abides in you. Then go ahead and take that first step toward the victory and success that God has in store for you!

PRAYER

Lord, show me how to overcome procrastination, laziness, and passivity. Help me to practice diligence and to tackle my obligations and tasks with vigor. Remind me that time is a precious resource that You have given us, and teach me to make the most of it. Thank You that my diligence will bring me heavenly and earthly rewards!

Who Needs Signs?

While the harpist was playing, the hand of the Lord came upon Elisha and he said, "This is what the Lord says: Make this valley full of ditches. For this is what the Lord says: You will see neither wind nor rain, yet this valley will be filled with water, and you, your cattle and your other animals will drink. This is an easy thing in the eyes of the Lord...."

2 KINGS 3:16-18

The kings of Israel, Judah, and Edom had united to attack Moab. After a seven-day march, the army had no water left for themselves or their animals. Their situation looked hopeless, and they were prepared to die. Then good King Jehoshaphat summoned Elisha, the prophet of God, who revealed the Lord's plan to perform a miracle on their behalf. To me, the most amazing part of this prophecy is the Lord saying, "You will see neither wind nor rain...." God is saying here, "You're not going to see any signs that a miracle is coming, but it's coming just the same." And not only was God going to do something that was virtually impossible, but He said, "This is an *easy* thing in the eyes of the Lord"!

I can think of so many times that I encountered challenges in my life—and though a part of me hoped God would intervene on my behalf—my faith faltered because I thought, *I don't see any signs that He's doing anything!* Are you waiting to see some evidence that God is working on your behalf in a situation? Are you waiting for the right phone call, letter in the mail, or other tangible evidence? Rest assured that it is an easy thing for God to come to your aid, even when signs that He will do so are virtually nonexistent!

PRAYER

Lord, forgive me when I've doubted You because I couldn't see any signs that You had plans to help me. Remind me that Your power and wisdom transcend my comprehension, and that Your love for me knows no bounds. Thank You that my deliverance is on its way—with or without signs!

LIVE ON PURPOSE TODAY

Believing that your deliverance is on the way with or without signs, lift your hands toward heaven even now and thank God for His goodness, for His mercy that endures forever, and for His mighty power at work in your behalf!

The Positive Power of Saying "No"

I recently read about a minister of the Gospel whose grateful congregation had sent him on a cruise. During his trip, he made the discovery that indulging his appetite had let it get totally out of control. I believe that reading about this man's experience was God's way of confirming that I was on the right track with my new eating habits. After having tried some popular diets that allowed the dieter to eat small quantities of anything they wanted—and after achieving dismal results—the Lord began instructing me to say "no" to many of my own natural desires, and to say "yes" to wiser ones. I discovered that the more I resisted having my own way where my eating was concerned, the more control I gained over my appetite. This control enabled me to not only lose weight, but to keep it off, as well.

The verses above from The Message Bible were life-changing for me. They made me realize how doing what I feel like doing all the time allows my natural desires to bully me. The more I give in to myself, the harder it becomes to discipline myself to do the right thing. On the other hand, the more I resist my natural impulses to indulge myself, the more control and freedom I gain—which is what God wants for His children. For instance, often when I go shopping and get the impulse to buy something, I begin to feel a "tension" between my flesh and my spirit. My flesh may say, "You can't pass this up—it's on sale!" But my spirit will give me a "check" about it, warning me to resist the urge to buy it. Then I have to decide which I want to please more—my spirit or my flesh. Either way, I will have to endure some kind of suffering. If I say "no" to myself, my flesh will suffer. If I say "yes" to myself, my spirit will suffer. I've discovered that if I can't get out of a situation without suffering somehow, it's best if I suffer in my flesh, rather than in my spirit. That's the attitude Jesus had, and that's what the verses above are referring to. The Living Bible puts it this way: "Since Christ suffered and underwent pain, you must have the same attitude he did; you must be ready to suffer, too. For remember, when your body suffers, sin loses its power, and you won't be spending the rest of your life chasing after evil desires, but will be anxious to do the will of God" (1 Peter 4:1,2 TLB). Every time we choose to suffer in our flesh rather than have our own way, sin's hold over us diminishes and it becomes easier to obey God. Before we accepted Christ as our Savior, there was no way we could have escaped the enslavement of sin. But with the gift of salvation comes the gift of the Holy Spirit and the power to

LIVE ON PURPOSE TODAY

Where have you been saying "yes," when you should have been saying "no"? When you have the answer to that question, find Scriptures that strengthen your "no," and remain steadfast in their support.

live a godly life in a fleshly body and a sinful world. God doesn't give us His Spirit just so we can live like the rest of the world. He gives us supernatural power so that we can say "no" to sin and live the abundant life that Jesus died to give us. Can we quench the Spirit's power working in us? Absolutely. If we continually ignore the Holy Spirit's conviction and leading, our hearts can become hardened and it can become increasingly difficult to hear God's "still, small voice." First Peter 1:14 in The Message Bible says, "Don't lazily slip back into those old grooves of evil, doing just what you feel like doing. You didn't know any better then; you do now." The truth is, you don't have to give in to your sinful nature anymore when it makes demands on you. The Bible says that you've been given a new nature (2 Cor. 5:17), and if you'll live your life with an attitude of total dependence upon God, you can enjoy the freedom that's found in doing His will. Don't let anyone tell you that doing what you feel like doing all the time will make you happy. The fact is that it will make you miserable. If you really want to enjoy your life and receive all the blessings God has for you, begin today to give yourself lots of daily doses of "No"!

PRAYER

Lord, when I'm tempted to have my own way against Your will, remind me of how my indulgence could harm my health, my finances, or my relationship with You or others. Help me to live a disciplined lifestyle so I can receive Your best in every area of my life. Thank You for the control and freedom that saying "no" to myself will bring!

Winning Battles God's Way

Do not say, "I'll pay you back for this wrong!"
Wait for the Lord, and he will deliver you.

PROVERBS 20:22

It seems that one of the hardest things for us to do is to wait for God to deliver us when we are victims of wrongdoing. Often our first reaction is to become angry, offended, or to retaliate somehow. Unfortunately, when we do that, we usually forfeit any help we might have gotten from the Lord. God taught me something about this through a painful lesson a few years ago.

My husband and I moved to a new home, and our two young sons began to get acquainted with the other kids in the neighborhood. At first, we were delighted that our children were making new friends, but it wasn't too long before we realized that the neighborhood kids were often mischievous, and even malicious at times. We finally told our sons that they were no longer allowed to associate with the neighborhood gang. My husband and I were as gracious about this as possible, but our neighbors became offended and their children began threatening our kids and attacking our home and property, doing serious damage. When trying to reason with them didn't work, we resorted to calling on the police for help. Not only did that fail to work, but it actually made the problem—and the attacks—worse. All this time I prayed and stood on God's promises for deliverance, while my husband became more and more bitter and contemplated taking matters into his own hands. Then one night we caught one of the

LIVE ON PURPOSE TODAY

Are you a victim of injustice? If so, make a concrete decision this very moment to follow God's lead in the matter. Father always knows best!

troublesome kids red-handed, and we filed charges against him. His parents came to my husband late that night, pleading with him to drop the charges against their son. I was amazed when my husband agreed and sent that family home, relieved and grateful. The police were not pleased with my husband's decision. They warned us that we had given up our only chance to stop the attacks on our home and family. But since that night we have lived here in peace. In addition, the Lord restored our home by causing our insurance company to put all new siding on our house.

Since then, whenever my family and I encounter injustice of any kind, we seek God's direction and we depend on Him to vindicate us. Yes, there are times we may have to take appropriate action—perhaps even legal action—but it should only be at God's direction and with His approval. Otherwise, it will be futile, or even disastrous. If you are in need of deliverance from injustice today, be encouraged by God's promise to you: "The Lord will vindicate his people and have compassion on his servants" (Ps. 135:14).

PRAYER

Lord, when I'm a victim of injustice, help me to seek Your direction above everyone else's. Show me when to take appropriate action and when to wait on You for deliverance. Teach me how to let You fight my battles for me so that I can gain the victory every time. Thank You for promising to be my Vindicator!

Following God's Peace

*Let the peace (soul harmony which comes) from Christ rule
(act as umpire continually) in your hearts, deciding
with finality all questions that arise in your minds....*

COLOSSIANS 3:15 AMP

Last summer I began experiencing some health problems that made it necessary for me to limit some of my activities, even with my doctor's care and prayer. My husband, Joe, and I already had a vacation planned with our oldest son and his wife. This trip involved a lengthy car ride, as well as a couple of nights in a hotel far from home. Even though I had misgivings about this trip, I pushed them aside as I thought about how disappointed my family would be if I told them I couldn't go. I prayed that the Lord would enable me to make this trip without any problems, and I asked my loved ones and fellow prayer warriors to keep me covered in prayer. Even so, within the first few hours of our departure, I got very sick, and I spent the rest of the day and night in bed in my hotel room. The next morning, as soon as I was able to travel, we headed back home, sorely disappointed that our trip had to be cut short.

After a lot of prayer and soul-searching, I realized that the Lord had given me plenty of warnings in advance that I should have canceled that trip, no matter how it might have disappointed my loved ones. Taking that trip was not a wise thing to do, and all the faith and prayer in the world were not going to change that. It was a painful, but very valuable, lesson for me. It made me realize that stepping out in faith is a wonderful thing—and something that God often asks and expects us to do. But it's also wonderful in His sight when we use godly wisdom, and when we recognize that we don't have peace about doing something we have prayed and sought God about. The Bible says, "Let the peace of God rule in your hearts" (Col. 3:15 NKJV). The Amplified translation puts it this way: "Let the peace (soul harmony which comes) from Christ rule (act as umpire continually) in your hearts, deciding with finality all questions that arise in your minds…." In my heart, I *knew* that going on that trip was not a good idea, but I did it anyway, and I suffered the consequences. (And so did my loved ones.) The fact is, when we don't have peace in our hearts about doing something, there's usually a good reason for it. It's true that the Lord will often ask us to step out in faith and do something that makes us fearful and anxious. But even during those times, we should have an inner peace that says—"Yes, this feels right. I do believe this is what God wants me to do." And the Lord's presence and power will be there to enable and sustain us.

LIVE ON PURPOSE TODAY

It's time to ask yourself a straightforward question: Is your heart pricking you in some way? Are you brushing aside any misgivings? Get quiet today and listen to your heart talk!

I've seen well-meaning Christians make horrendous mistakes they could have avoided if they had just used some godly wisdom. Somehow, they've gotten the notion that whenever God asks them to step out in faith, He's always going to lead them to do something that is irrational or unreasonable. They seem to have forgotten that the Bible says, "Wisdom is supreme; therefore, get wisdom. Though it cost all you have, get understanding" (Prov. 4:7). The Living Bible puts it this way: "Getting wisdom is the most important thing you can do! And with your wisdom, develop common sense and good judgment." When we act in faith, God doesn't expect us to bypass our intellect. He will still expect us to seek Him for godly wisdom and discernment in everything we do. That's why Scripture says, "If you want to know what God wants you to do, ask Him, and He will gladly tell you, for He is always ready to give a bountiful supply of wisdom to all who ask Him; He will not resent it" (James 1:5 TLB). The next time you're faced with a decision to make, I hope you'll rely on God's peace—as well as His wisdom—to guide you. For it's in the paths of peace that you'll find His very best blessings!

PRAYER

Lord, whenever I need to make a decision, remind me to turn to You for godly wisdom and guidance. When I sense an absence of peace about a certain course of action, remind me to pause and wait for further instructions from You. Thank You, Lord, that as I follow Your peace, Your blessings will follow me!

An Example of the Abundant Life

"I came that they may have and enjoy life, and have
it in abundance (to the full, till it overflows)."

JOHN 10:10 AMP

I have a dear friend, Peggy, who is showered with blessings wherever she goes. I have never known anyone who was living the "abundant life" quite like this dear lady is. She is a true inspiration to me and to countless other believers, and I admire her immensely. We were chatting together the other day, and we began discussing what it could be that enabled Peggy to be blessed "exceedingly abundantly above all that we ask or think" (Eph. 3:20 NKJV). We decided that one possible reason was the fact that Peggy always *expects* to be blessed. I've often heard her say, "God loves an expectant heart," and I believe this is true. She says that she always holds her "umbrella" upside down to catch showers of blessings from heaven. She has no problem receiving from the Lord, as some of us do, so she is always ready and willing to accept the good things He offers.

Peggy prays BIG prayers. She sees her God as a BIG God—an all-powerful God, with whom nothing is impossible. (Luke 1:37.) She doesn't put limits or restrictions on God. She gives Him plenty of room to work in every matter she prays about. And she always has a positive outlook, no matter how hopeless a situation seems. She truly believes that no matter how bleak the circumstances appear, God will turn them into good for her and other believers. (Rom. 8:28.)

Another reason that Peggy is so blessed may be because she believes God *desires* to bless her, simply because she has a personal relationship with Him, not because she does everything right. Peggy is not perfect. But she is the perfect example of someone who is truly "abiding" in Christ, and who is living in union with Him every moment of every day. (John 15:5.) Peggy prays about everything. (Phil. 4:6.) She doesn't view any matter as too small or insignificant to bring to the Lord in prayer, and she does her best to be sensitive and obedient to His leading at all times. When she does sin, she is quick to repent and receive God's forgiveness. (1 John 1:9.) She doesn't dwell on her mistakes, and it is very rare when she allows herself to be overwhelmed by guilt and condemnation. Peggy's relationship with the Lord is the most important thing in her life, and she is committed to doing whatever she needs to in order to maintain a vibrant and intimate relationship with Him.

LIVE ON PURPOSE TODAY

Can you think of someone with whom you've only exchanged pleasantries, yet you've thought, *Hmm, I see God in this person, and I seem drawn. I'd like to get to know him better.* Then don't delay! Consider inviting the individual for coffee or lunch—knowing that God arranges divine connections in your behalf.

Perhaps most importantly, Peggy is always quick to give God the thanks and the praise for all of her blessings. (Eph. 5:20.) She feels that more believers would be blessed if they would acknowledge to the Lord—and others—that every good thing that comes their way is from Him. (James 1:17.) Even if a blessing that she didn't pray for or expect comes her way, she promptly and sincerely thanks God for it. She never uses rationale or reasoning to "explain away" the good things she receives daily. She always maintains "an attitude of gratitude," and the Lord continually honors and rewards her for it.

When someone comments on Peggy's extraordinarily blessed life in her presence, she always tells them, "God is no respecter of persons. What He does for me, He'll do for you!" Peggy doesn't just say that to try to make people feel better—she knows that God says it in His Word, so it must be true. (Acts 10:34.) She has a sincere love for the Scriptures, and she takes every promise from God personally. If you don't have someone in your life like Peggy to encourage and inspire you, I hope you'll pray and ask the Lord to send you someone. Better yet, ask God to help *you* be a shining example of someone who is living the abundant life in Christ!

PRAYER

Lord Jesus, You said that You came so that I could live the abundant life, and I ask You to teach me how to do exactly that. Surround me with people who will challenge and inspire me to live a blessed life that will draw others to You. Expand my vision, and enable me to see You as the big, loving, and giving God You are. Thank You, Lord, that what You've done for Peggy, You will do for me!

Strength in Adversity

If you falter in times of trouble, how small is your strength!

PROVERBS 24:10

The Lord often shows me this verse when I'm going through difficult times. It's one of those "ouch" verses in the Bible, and it always convicts me when I see it. The Living Bible version says, "You are a poor specimen if you can't stand the pressure of adversity." God said basically the same thing to the prophet Jeremiah when he was complaining to the Lord about the injustices he had to deal with. "If you have raced with men on foot and they have worn you out, how can you compete with horses? If you stumble in safe country, how will you manage in the thickets by the Jordan?" (Jer. 12:5). In other words, "If you think this is bad, how are you going to handle it when things really get tough?" One reason why God wants us to be strong in times of trouble is because He wants to use us to advance the work of His kingdom. He can't do that if we fall apart every time we face a crisis in our lives. Can you imagine a commander putting weak and fearful soldiers on the front lines? Not only would his men get slaughtered, but he wouldn't have much chance of victory.

What does the Bible say about strength, and what can we do to appropriate the strength God wants us to demonstrate? Scripture says that the Lord Himself is our strength (Ps. 18:1), and we can declare Him as our strength, as David did. It says that the people who "know their God" (in a personal way) "shall be strong and carry out great exploits" (Dan. 11:32 NKJV). It also says that unconfessed sin can "sap our strength" (Ps. 32:4), so admitting our sin to God and receiving His forgiveness can restore us. The Bible tells us that "the joy of the Lord is our strength" (Neh. 8:10), so sadness and depression can

LIVE ON PURPOSE TODAY

Praise God and thank Him today for His goodness and His mighty power. As the Lord becomes magnified in your eyes, adversity will become minimized, and renewed strength will be yours.

make us weak. And we're told that we are strengthened when we trust in God and put our hope in Him. (Isa. 30:15; 40:31.) We can pray for strength, and we can stand on the many promises in God's Word concerning strength. In Psalm 86:16, David prayed, "Grant your strength to your servant." And in Psalm 18:32, David declared, "It is God who arms me with strength." The apostle Paul wrote, "I can do all things through Christ who strengthens me" (Phil. 4:13 NKJV), so we can be sure that God will give us the strength we need to handle all that He calls us to. Paul also writes, "Be strong in the Lord and in his mighty power" (Eph. 6:10), so we know that being strong involves our will and is something that we're capable of because of our relationship with God. And I have discovered that in times of crisis and weakness, praising God and giving Him thanks can build us up and strengthen us like nothing else can. May this promise from God encourage you today: "I command you—be strong and courageous! Do not be afraid or discouraged. For the Lord your God is with you wherever you go"! (Joshua 1:9 NLT).

PRAYER

Lord, in times of trouble, show me how to stand strong so that I won't falter. Fill me with Your joy to give me strength, and help me to put my trust in You. Guard me from any unconfessed sin that could weaken me or hinder my fellowship with You. Let David's declaration be mine each day—"I love You, O Lord, my Strength!" (Ps. 18:1).

God's Purpose in Testing Us

Remember how the Lord your God led you all the way in the desert these forty years, to humble you and to test you in order to know what was in your heart, whether or not you would keep his commands.... He gave you manna to eat in the desert, something your fathers had never known, to humble and to test you so that in the end it might go well with you.

DEUTERONOMY 8:2,16

If you tell some Christians that you believe God tests us sometimes, they get mad. Yet if you read enough of the Bible, you can't deny that it's true. The above verses are abundantly clear. God tested the Israelites in the wilderness to humble them and to find out what was in their hearts, whether they would obey Him or not. In verse 16, the Lord reveals His purpose, "so that in the end it might go well with you." God doesn't test us because He's mean and sadistic. He tests us because He loves us and He knows that trials can stretch us and make us grow. Why is the Lord so interested in our spiritual growth? There are probably many reasons, but a few I can think of offhand are that He can bless us more, we can be a greater blessing to others, and God can use us more for His glory. If we look at Job, some might say that it was Satan that did the testing, and technically, they'd be right. But it's also true that it was God who allowed Job to be tested. God was convinced that His servant would be faithful to Him no matter what, and He was right. And though Job was already "the greatest man among all the people of the East," the Lord rewarded Job with even greater blessings after his test than before.

Abraham was another man whom God loved and tested. Hebrews 11:17 says, "By faith Abraham, when God tested him,

LIVE ON PURPOSE TODAY

With great resolve, endure hardness as a good soldier and purpose to pass your test with flying colors so you won't need to face it again.

offered Isaac as a sacrifice." Like Job, Abraham remained faithful to God in good times and bad, and the Lord kept His promise to "bless him and make his name great." If you study the lives of the people of the Bible, you discover that the ones God blessed and used the most were often the ones He tested the most. And many times, the greatest tests came right before the greatest blessings. Maybe you feel like you're in the desert of testing right now. Perhaps God wants to use you in a special way, and He is calling you to a higher level of faith and obedience. Instead of resisting the stretching pain of your trials, if you'll settle down and determine to pass the test by walking in obedience to God, not only will your faith become stronger, but God will reward you somehow. He may give you greater responsibilities or opportunities. He may bless you with more prosperity or with new social contacts. Rest assured that when God allows you to undergo tests and trials, it's because He loves you and wants to bless you. I pray the next time you travel through the desert of testing, your declaration of faith will be the same as Job's: "When he has tested me, I will come forth as gold"! (Job 23:10).

PRAYER

Lord, though I don't fully understand why You allow us to go through tests and trials, I believe with all my heart that You are good and that You love me. Help me to pass my tests with a good attitude so that You can bless me the way You want to, and so that You can use me for Your glory. Thank You for the rewards You have in store for me!

God's Umbrella
of Protection

"He's (God's) a rich mine of common sense for those who live well, a personal bodyguard to the candid and sincere."

PROVERBS 2:7 MESSAGE

Recently, a young teen wrote and poured her heart out to me, about how she had drifted away from God and how her life was slowly unraveling as a result. She was hanging around with the wrong kind of friends, and the negative impact they were having on her life was becoming more and more evident in her own behavior. No matter how she struggled to maintain her identity in Christ, she felt herself being pulled further and further away from God. I recognized her letter as a cry for help, but I didn't realize how desperate a cry it was until a few days later, when her mother wrote me and described the tragic incident that had befallen her daughter the night before.

This experience reminded me of a powerful demonstration that I witnessed in church years ago. The pastor was holding an umbrella over his head, saying that God's protection was like a spiritual covering over us, as long as we were walking in His will and His ways. But then the pastor stepped out from under the umbrella, emphasizing that we remove ourselves from God's protective covering whenever we step outside of His will. I believe that this is exactly what happened to the young girl who wrote me. While she was devoted to God, she was in a place of safety and blessing. But when she turned her back on God and His guidelines for living, she placed herself in harm's way, and the devil did the rest. Jesus said that He came to give us abundant life, while Satan "comes only to steal and kill and destroy" (John 10:10). When we walk away from God and His will for us, we give the devil permission to come into our lives and do us harm.

Scripture indicates that angelic protection is available to those who devote themselves to the Lord. The Amplified version of the following verse brings out this truth beautifully: "For He will give His angels [especial] charge over you to accompany and defend and preserve you in all your ways [of obedience and service]" (Ps. 91:11 AMP). Throughout the pages of the Bible, God's people are promised angelic protection. But we can't expect God to give us the same degree of protection when we're walking in disobedience and "doing our own thing." In order to enjoy the greatest level of divine protection, we need to have a reverential fear of the Lord. Scripture says, "The angel of the Lord encamps around those who fear Him [who revere and worship Him with awe] and each of them He delivers" (Ps. 34:7 AMP).

LIVE ON PURPOSE TODAY

Now that you've prayed and your heart is quiet before the Lord, answer a few important questions for yourself. Are you in fellowship with the Lord? Are you following His will for your life? Do you regularly obey promptings and warnings from the Holy Spirit?

The thing that impresses me most about this girl's sad story is that I believe God had warned her that trouble was headed her way, if she continued to drift away from Him. Her letter to me and her cry for help, just days before tragedy struck, are proof that the

Lord had been dealing with her about her disobedience. I've heard my husband say countless times that "God always gives us warnings," and there are many verses in the Bible that confirm this fact. Job 33:14-18 says, "In a dream, for instance, a vision at night, when men and women are deep in sleep, fast asleep in their beds—God opens their ears and impresses them with warnings, to turn them back from something bad they're planning, from some reckless choice, and keep them from an early grave, from the river of no return" (MESSAGE). When we are on the path of destruction, the Lord will go to great lengths to get us back on the right track. But if we continually resist His Spirit's promptings, our hearts can become hardened, and we can easily miss His loving cues.

Today, if you sense that you are on a path leading away from God, I urge you to stop in your tracks and cry out to Him for help, before it's too late. May this precious promise from the Lord encourage your heart today: "'If you'll hold on to Me for dear life,' says God, 'I'll get you out of any trouble. I'll give you the best of care, if you'll only get to know and trust Me.'" (Ps. 91:14 MESSAGE).

PRAYER

Lord, I humble myself before You today, and I ask You to make it clear to me if there is any sin in my life that You would like me to deal with at this time. Please give me a tender heart and a tender conscience, and make me sensitive and obedient to Your Spirit's leading in all things. Thank You, Lord, that as I continually submit to Your will and ways, I will remain under Your covering of protection, safety, and blessing!

He Lifts Us Up

The Lord lifts up those who are bowed down.

PSALM 146:8

I know what it's like to be "bowed down"—to feel beaten, depressed, weighed down, and defeated. If you've ever felt like that, this promise from God is for you, as much as it is for me. Sometimes our problems seem so overwhelming that we feel we're being crushed under the weight of them. Psalm 145:14 NLT says, "The Lord helps the fallen and lifts up those bent beneath their loads." It's never God's will for us to carry our own burdens, and His burden-bearing power is always available to us. But often we have to do our part in the process. The Bible tells us to cast our cares on the Lord. (Ps. 55:22; 1 Peter 5:7.) So we need to give our burdens to God in prayer, and then trust Him to sustain us according to His promise. James 4:10 NLT says, "When you bow down before the Lord and admit your dependence on Him, He will lift you up and give you honor." God is eager to rescue us, but many times He will wait for us to humble ourselves before Him and confess our need for Him. "I need You, Lord; please help me," is a simple but powerful prayer. In Psalm 3:3, David declares, "You are a shield around me, O Lord; you bestow glory on me and lift up my head." Many times, as in this verse and the previous one, "lifting up" is associated with our receiving glory and honor from the Lord, as well as comfort and deliverance. God isn't just interested in helping us live burden-free lives; He wants to help us live lives filled with success and victory!

Job 22:29 says, "When men are brought low and you say, 'Lift them up!' then He will save the downcast." God has promised that our prayers can make a difference in the lives of those who are discouraged and depressed. Likewise, when we are the ones in need of a lift, it may be wise for us to seek out fellow believers who will intercede for us with the Lord. Ask God who you should request prayer support from, and then don't hesitate to receive the help He offers. When I go through difficult times that threaten to shake my faith, I remind myself of two things that I know without a doubt: (1) God is a good God, and (2) He loves us with a perfect love. This helps me to deal with the unanswered questions. We don't often think of an all-powerful God suffering along with us, but look at this verse in Isaiah 63:9 NLT: "In all their suffering He also suffered, and He personally rescued them. In His love and mercy He redeemed them. He lifted them up and carried them through all the years." I'm so thankful that we serve a God who feels our pain and desires only good for us. If you're in need of a lift today, let me encourage you to share your true feelings with the Lord. If your faith is faltering, be honest with Him and ask for His help. And have a good cry when you feel the need. God gave us tears for a reason, and they can be very healing. Stand on this promise from the Lord today: "You have allowed me to suffer much hardship, but you will restore me to life again and lift me up from the depths of the earth. You will restore me to even greater honor and comfort me once again"! (Ps. 71:20,21 NLT).

LIVE ON PURPOSE TODAY

Are you feeling bowed down? If so, pick up the phone and call that one the Lord prompts you to seek prayer support from. Don't delay, and help will be on its way!

PRAYER

Lord, when I'm feeling bowed down, help me to turn to You in humility and honesty, and lift me up the way that only You can. Show me whom I should seek out for prayer support, and deliver me from the negative feelings that would hinder me from receiving their help. I don't just want to survive, Lord—I want to thrive! Thank You for lifting me up, and giving me honor and glory in Your name!

Don't Get Offended

A man's wisdom gives him patience;
it is to his glory to overlook an offense.

PROVERBS 19:11

Are you easily offended? If you are, you have plenty of company these days. Our society has made becoming offended a national pastime. It's almost as if we've made offense a virtue today. One example of this is the prevalence of "road rage." One driver gets offended with another, and what began as a minor altercation can escalate into a major conflict. But that's not God's way. The verse above tells us that the honorable thing for us to do in these situations is to overlook the offense. If you want to defuse a volatile situation, refuse to become offended. Yes, you may have been wronged. And your feelings might have been hurt. But if you are a believer, God Himself has promised to be your Vindicator, and He will deal with those who treat you unfairly. (Ps. 135:14.) Your job is to handle situations like these His way, not the world's way. Psalm 119:165 AMP says, "Great peace have they who love Your law; nothing shall offend them or make them stumble." If we are lovers and doers of God's Word, we will walk in peace and we will not be easily offended. When the apostle Paul is describing the God-kind of love that believers are to demonstrate, he says, "It is not rude, it is not self-seeking, it is not easily angered, it keeps no record of wrongs" (1 Cor. 13:5). The next time you are tempted to take offense at something someone says to you, pray and ask the Lord, "Is there any truth to this, Lord? Do I need to make some changes here?" Then be honest with yourself and God, and let Him deal with you, if necessary.

Proverbs 18:19 says, "An offended brother is more unyielding than a fortified city." Is there someone in your life, like a family member, who gets offended easily, and whom you have to deal with on a regular basis? People like these can be difficult to get along with because when they take offense, they refuse to listen to reason or to yield to attempts to make amends. We may not always be able to avoid offending these people, but there are a couple of things we can do. We can pray for them, and we can refuse to become offended ourselves. The reason taking offense is displeasing to God is that it's destructive to relationships. It divides people and causes conflict. It can break up families, friendships, and even churches. It's one of Satan's most valuable weapons against God's kingdom, and as believers, we are to be aware of his tactics so that we won't become his victims. (2 Cor. 2:11.) Proverbs 17:9 AMP says, "He who covers and forgives an offense seeks love, but he who repeats or harps on a matter separates even close friends." Every time we forgive an offense, we are preserving our relationships and slamming the door in the devil's face. Most of all, we are pleasing and glorifying the One who deserves our very best!

LIVE ON PURPOSE TODAY

Determine to see just how many doors you can slam in the devil's face today by forgiving every offense that comes your way!

PRAYER

Lord, You know better than anyone how many opportunities to take offense I encounter each day. I ask that You give me the grace I need to resist becoming offended in these situations. Make me an example and an inspiration to others. Deal with me when I'm in the wrong and I need to make some changes. When I suffer hurt, heal and comfort me. Thank You that by Your grace, I shall walk in peace!

Sin: It's All in Your Mind

For though we walk in the flesh, we do not war according to the flesh. For the weapons of our warfare are not carnal but mighty in God for pulling down strongholds, casting down arguments and every high thing that exalts itself against the knowledge of God, bringing every thought into captivity to the obedience of Christ.

2 CORINTHIANS 10:3-5 NKJV

These verses reveal that if we are going to defeat Satan and live godly lives in a fallen world, we are going to have to win the battle in our minds. If you are struggling with some kind of sin right now, in order to overcome it, you will have to take captive every thought that precedes the sin. If you don't, you will eventually act upon those thoughts. There's no way you can commit a sin without thinking about it first. When the thought of sinning is first introduced, if you decide it's not an option, you won't act upon it. Studying Scripture is essential because our minds need to be renewed. If they aren't, we will not be able to reject the thoughts we need to. Romans 12:2 says, "Do not conform any longer to the pattern of this world, but be transformed by the renewing of your mind. Then you will be able to test and approve what God's will is—his good, pleasing and perfect will."

Every time you resist temptation, your flesh (sinful nature) gets weaker and your spirit gets stronger. That's why every time you resist, it gets easier to resist. But every time you sin, it can become easier to sin. First Peter 4:1-2 says, "Since Christ suffered for us in the flesh, arm yourselves with the same mind, for he who has suffered in the flesh has ceased from sin, that he no longer should live the rest of his

LIVE ON PURPOSE TODAY

Take thoughts captive today by silencing them with God's Word. Find Scriptures that offer an antidote to the sin that plagues you. For instance, if you're fearful, find Scriptures on God's perfect love which casts out fear. The Bible will infuse you with strength and program you with change!

time in the flesh for the lusts of men, but for the will of God." If you're going to overcome the sin in your life, you're going to have to suffer in the flesh. You'll have to think like Christ and be determined to do the will of God, instead of having your own way. Your flesh won't like it, and it will be tough at first, but it will get easier every time you succeed. Colossians 3:2 says, "Set your minds on things above, not on earthly things." You'll need to make a conscious effort to keep your mind off of worldly things. Here again, knowledge of God's Word is essential, as is prayer. You may have to do a lot of crying out to God in the beginning, but that's okay. He wants to help you win this battle. Finally, "walk by the Spirit, and you will not carry out the desire of the flesh" (Gal. 5:16). You must determine to live your life being sensitive and obedient to the promptings of the Holy Spirit. This war is winnable. Take your stand and be victorious!

PRAYER

Lord, I want so much to do Your will. Teach me to renew my mind and walk by Your Spirit. Help me to spend time in Your Word and in prayer so that I will not be a pushover for Satan. Show me how to capture every thought and make it obedient to Christ. When I do sin, help me to be quick to repent, and to renew my resolve to get back into the battle. Thank You that You are on my side, and with Your help, I can't lose!

An Invitation to Criticism

For I endure scorn for Your sake, and shame covers my face.
I am a stranger to my brothers, an alien to my own
mother's sons; for zeal for Your house consumes me,
and the insults of those who insult You fall on me.

PSALM 69:7-9 NIV

For me, these are some of the saddest verses in Scripture. The Bible says that God called David a man after His own heart. Yet many of the verses penned by this warrior-king reveal that he was often insulted and rejected because of his passion for God, even by his family and friends. Second Samuel 6 records that when David brought the ark of the covenant into Jerusalem, he "danced before the Lord with all his might," in celebration (v. 14). It says that when his wife, Michal, saw David's unrestrained enthusiasm for the Lord, she "despised him in her heart" (v. 16). When she criticized her husband for his public display of emotion, not only did David not apologize for it, but he informed her that he would become "even more undignified than this" in honor of the Lord (v. 22). The last verse in the chapter reveals that it is Michal, not David, who is judged by God, as she remains childless for the rest of her life.

In the Gospel of John, we see the same phrase, "zeal for Your house consumes me," attributed to Jesus when He rids the temple of moneychangers (John 2:17). When we display a Holy Spirit-inspired passion (or "zeal") for God, we are modeling the kind of devotion that the Son of God and David demonstrated. And just as they were often insulted and rejected, we will be, too. In Matthew 5:11-12 (MESSAGE), Jesus tells us how to react in those times:

LIVE ON PURPOSE TODAY

If you've suffered criticism, be now encouraged and persevere today. Follow Jesus' own instructions and count yourself blessed if you've been put down. Focus on the applause you're receiving from heaven!

"Count yourselves blessed every time people put you down or throw you out or speak lies about you to discredit Me. What it means is that the truth is too close for comfort and they are uncomfortable. You can be glad when that happens—give a cheer, even!—for though they don't like it, I do! And all heaven applauds." We can take comfort in the fact that our devotion delights the heart of God. In Romans 12:11, Paul urges us to "never be lacking in zeal, but keep your spiritual fervor, serving the Lord." Don't ever be ashamed because you serve God with enthusiasm. Isaiah 51:7-8 says, "Hear Me, you who know what is right, you people who have My law in your hearts: Do not fear the reproach of men or be terrified by their insults. For the moth will eat them up like a garment; the worm will devour them like wool." Our God is merciful, but He is also committed to His servants. Forgive and pray for the people who insult you, then let God deal with them. Rest in this promise from the Lord today: "Be happy if you are cursed and insulted for being a Christian, for when that happens the Spirit of God will come upon you with great glory"! (1 Peter 4:14 TLB).

PRAYER

Lord, teach me to serve You with a Spirit-led passion. When I'm criticized because of it, comfort me and help me to respond with a Christlike attitude. Guard me from feeling ashamed for displaying a holy zeal for You. May my devotion always invite applause from heaven!

In Times of Betrayal and Injustice

Then the king said to Zadok, "Take the ark of God back into the city. If I find favor in the Lord's eyes, he will bring me back and let me see it and his dwelling place again. But if he says, 'I am not pleased with you,' then let him do to me whatever seems good to him."

2 SAMUEL 15:25,26

The above verses are from the Bible account of Absalom's plot to take the throne away from his father, King David. When Absalom leads a widespread revolt against his father, instead of David crushing the rebellion, he flees Jerusalem with those who have remained loyal to him. If you know anything about David, you know he was no coward. Many historians consider him the most courageous and successful warrior of all time. Yet here, he chooses to leave his beloved city behind so that it would be spared from certain destruction. While it takes great courage to stand and fight, sometimes it takes even greater courage to walk away and leave things in God's hands. These verses reveal the magnitude of David's faith in God. When faced with betrayal, injustice, and disappointment, he entrusts himself to the Lord and says basically, "Thy will be done."

Perhaps you've been in David's place at sometime in your life. If you've ever been passed over when you believed you deserved a promotion, you have an idea of how David must have felt. If the position at church or in school you thought you

LIVE ON PURPOSE TODAY

If you stick with God, you'll always come out on top. So, the next time unfairness and injustice rear their ugly heads, remind yourself that God is on your side. He will always take you to victory!

deserved went to someone else, you can empathize with him. If you've ever felt betrayed or unjustly mistreated by family members, you've been in David's shoes. David was a faithful servant of the Lord, and he loved God with all his heart. He made mistakes, and he suffered the conse-quences. He trusted God in the best of times and the worst of times. And even when his own son rebelled against him, David entrusted himself to the Lord, and God eventually restored him to his rightful place as king. First Peter 2:23 says that when Jesus was treated unjustly, "he entrusted himself to him who judges justly." Considering the outcome of their lives, do you think that David or the Master ever regretted leaving themselves in God's hands? No way. Next time you are confronted with injustice and disappointment, if you'll entrust yourself to the Lord, when all is said and done, He will honor you and lift you up!

PRAYER

Lord, I know that serving You doesn't guarantee that I'll always be treated fairly. But sometimes when I'm faced with unfairness, the hurt and bewilderment are just too much for me to bear. In times like these, remind me that Your Word says You are a "God of Justice." And give me the reassurance that You will work even my trials out for my good. Thank You that You are on my side!

The Costs and Rewards
of Discipleship

> *Peter said to [Jesus], "We have left everything to follow you!"*
> *"I tell you the truth," Jesus replied, "no one who has left home or*
> *brothers or sisters or mother or father or children or fields for me*
> *and the gospel will fail to receive a hundred times as much in this*
> *present age (homes, brothers, sisters, mothers, children and fields—*
> *and with them, persecutions) and in the age to come, eternal life."*
>
> MARK 10:28-30

These verses should be a great comfort to those of us who have made sacrifices to follow the Savior and do His will. Throughout the Gospels, Jesus warns us that those who want to be His disciples should be prepared to make sacrifices. In Luke 14:33, He says, "Any of you who does not give up everything he has cannot be my disciple." Of course, most of us will not be asked to give up everything we have, but Jesus is referring to a certain mindset and attitude of the heart here. God wants us to be willing to surrender to Him all that He asks us to. And He wants us to know that discipleship can be costly. But serving God has its rewards, too. Look at the above verses again. Jesus says that no matter who or what we give up, we will receive a hundredfold return in this lifetime, as well as eternal life in the next. The Savior is assuring us here that we can't outgive God! And the more costly the sacrifice, the greater the reward.

The apostle Paul knew what it was like to make great sacrifices for God. He was a well-respected Pharisee when the Lord

LIVE ON PURPOSE TODAY

Is God asking you to give up something today? Will you do it? Remember, it doesn't cost to serve God—it pays.

called him into service on the road to Damascus. He sacrificed his reputation, his family, his friends, and eventually his life, to follow Jesus. He endured endless persecution, as well as repeated beatings and imprisonments. Yet look at these verses he wrote in Philippians 3:7-8:

"But whatever was to my profit I now consider loss for the sake of Christ. What is more, I consider everything a loss compared to the surpassing greatness of knowing Christ Jesus my Lord, for whose sake I have lost all things. I consider them rubbish, that I may gain Christ...." What is God asking you to give up today? A relationship that is not in His will for you? A job that is separating you from His greatest blessings? Some form of entertainment that is detrimental to your relationship with Him? Whatever it is, if you will surrender it to the Lord, He will reward you in unimaginable ways. After all, "No eye has seen, no ear has heard, no mind has conceived what God has prepared for those who love him"! (1 Cor. 2:9).

PRAYER

Lord, it is my heart's desire to be Your disciple and follow You. Give me the grace I need to wholeheartedly surrender to You all that I have and all that I am. Help me to make the sacrifices I need to so that nothing and no one will ever come between us. Thank You for rewarding me with abundant blessings and a closer relationship with You!

The Faith of Abraham

*Against all hope, Abraham in hope believed and so became
the father of many nations, just as it had been said to him....*

ROMANS 4:18

God has used this verse countless times to encourage me
when I've been faced with hopeless situations and was
tempted to lose heart. I find Abraham's example of faith
so profoundly inspiring, and it never ceases to give me hope. The
phrase, "Against all hope, Abraham in hope believed," speaks of
the kind of faith that defies hopelessness. Abraham was keenly
aware of his doubtful situation. In fact, the next verse confirms
this: "Without weakening in his faith, he faced the fact that his
body was as good as dead—since he was about a hundred years
old—and that Sarah's womb was also dead" (Rom. 4:19).
Abraham was not in denial. He clearly was facing the facts of his
situation, yet Scripture says that he did this "without weakening
in his faith." No wonder God honored this man the way He did.
How many of us in Abraham's situation would have held on to the
promise of God? Some believers think that you have to be in a
kind of state of denial in order to receive the miraculous in hopeless situations, but I don't think that's true. Real faith says, "I
know my situation looks hopeless, but I also know that I belong
to a God who has a history of moving mountains for His children,
and I'm keeping my eyes on Him!" You don't have to know *how*
God's going to keep His promise to you; all you have to know is
that He will do it!

Romans 4:20 says, "Yet [Abraham] did not waver through unbelief regarding the promise of God, but was strengthened in his faith and gave glory to God, being fully persuaded that God had power to do what he had promised." The Message Bible puts it this way: "Abraham didn't tiptoe around God's promise asking cautiously skeptical questions. He plunged into the promise and came up strong, ready for God." One thing is certain—a lack of faith will make us waver. It will cause us to doubt God's ability and willingness to do the impossible on our behalf. It's God's desire that we be "fully persuaded" that He is able to work wonders in our lives, even when our circumstances are screaming defeat at us. Notice that this verse reveals that Abraham "gave glory to God" while he was waiting for God to fulfill His promise to him. Abraham didn't wait until the manifestation of his miracle to give thanks and praise to the Lord—that doesn't take much faith. But he began thanking God in advance, strengthening his own faith in the process. The Living Bible brings this out best when it says, "He praised God for this blessing even before it happened." Scripture goes on to say that it's "those who are of the faith of Abraham" who receive the promises of God (Rom. 4:16). If we want to receive the kind of blessings that Abraham did, we need to demonstrate the kind of faith that he did. That means we will have to push logic and reasoning aside

LIVE ON PURPOSE TODAY

Follow the example of Abraham today by giving glory to God because you are fully persuaded that He will keep His promises to you. No matter the situation or circumstance you face, continually thank God that He's at work in your behalf.

and focus on God and His promises. If you're a child of God and you'll follow Abraham's example, rest assured that what God did for this great man of faith, He'll do for you, too!

PRAYER

Lord, teach me to have the faith of Abraham. When I encounter "hopeless" situations, help me to keep my eyes on You, instead of on my circumstances. Remind me not to wait for the manifestation of my miracle before I give You thanks and praise. Thank You that as I follow Abraham's example, I will impact the lives of others and glorify You!

Shake It Off!

> *"If anyone will not welcome you or listen to your words, shake the dust off your feet when you leave that home or town."*
>
> MATTHEW 10:14

The Lord brought the above verse to my remembrance recently, when I was doing my best to give a loved one some godly advice. I confess that it grieves my heart when I see people I care about casting aside God's will for them and choosing to go their own way. Since I surrendered my life to the Lord years ago and have gotten a taste of the abundant life that Jesus spoke of, I long to see others turn their own lives over to Him and experience the same blessings. But sometimes, no matter how I try to reach out to others with the love and grace of God, my words go unheeded. Maybe you've felt the same way about some of the people in your own life. It's not easy for us to watch loved ones make wrong choices, especially when they result in serious consequences. If we're not careful, we can allow anger, bitterness, or resentment to worm their way into our hearts.

On this particular occasion, the Lord gave me my own personal paraphrase of His words in Matthew 10:14. He told me, "If someone will not listen to you, shake it off and move on!" And I desperately needed to hear those words. Instead of letting the matter go and leaving this person in God's hands, I was holding on to my frustration, my helplessness, and my resentment. And I felt as though all of my peace and joy—gifts that Jesus died to give me—had flown out the window. That's when I turned to the Lord in heartfelt repentance and asked Him to help me "shake off" the negative emotions that threatened to overwhelm me, and He didn't hesitate to answer that prayer.

Notice that Jesus didn't tell His disciples—"When people don't listen to you, I want you to whine, complain, get depressed and angry. I want you to focus on their disobedience and how they're ruining their own lives. I want you to keep thinking about all of the blessings they're forfeiting because they refuse to walk in the good plans I have for them." No, Jesus said, "Shake it off and move on!" The Savior knows that it will do us *no good* to waste time fretting over the wrong choices that others make. All it will do is hinder our prayers for these people and make us ineffective witnesses for God.

I like the way the Message Bible translates Jesus' words in Matthew 10:14. It says, "If they don't welcome you, quietly withdraw. Don't make a scene. Shrug your shoulders and be on your way." Even if our words fall on deaf ears and we decide to walk away, we still have powerful spiritual weapons that can make a difference. We can persist in prayer for these people, and we can consistently set a Christlike example for them, planting seeds in their lives that will eventually produce a heavenly harvest.

LIVE ON PURPOSE TODAY

Have you experienced feelings of anger and resentment towards a friend or family member because they wouldn't heed your advice? "Shake off" those negative feelings right now! Ask God to forgive you, then pray that He will send someone else along their path to minister to them.

The next time you minister words of wisdom to someone and they "blow you off," don't forget that that's your cue to *"shake it off"*!

PRAYER

Lord, forgive me for the times I reacted badly when I ministered to others and didn't get the response that I desired. Teach me how to be more Christlike in this area, and help me to do my part in the process. Remind me that it's never Your will for me to hang on to negative emotions that will only hinder my prayers and my fellowship with You. Thank You that as I walk as Jesus did, You will use me to touch and change lives for Your glory!

Turning Adversities
Into Advantages

I am going to keep on being glad, for I know that as
you pray for me, and as the Holy Spirit helps me,
this is all going to turn out for my good.

PHILIPPIANS 1:19 TLB

I have many favorite Bible verses, but the one above holds a special place in my heart because it has gotten me through a lot of hard times. The most recent example was when I broke a tooth so badly that I had to have it ground down and capped. I had never had such extensive dental work done before, and I was really downhearted about it. The temporary cap the dentist gave me was unattractive, and I had to wait several weeks for my permanent one. I sought the Lord in prayer, and I asked some of my faith-filled loved ones to pray for me. When my permanent cap finally arrived, I wasn't happy with it, and I asked my dentist to make some adjustments to improve its appearance. That meant that I would have to wait a few more weeks before the work would be completed. As I felt my faith beginning to fade, I prayed for more grace, and I asked the Lord to bring good out of this whole ordeal somehow. When the dentist's office called to say that my new cap was ready, I was so nervous that I could hardly pray. As I drove to the office and stepped toward the door, all I could say was, "This is all going to turn out for my good!" I'm happy to report that everything went smoothly at the dentist's office that day. Not only did God restore my smile, but He made it better than ever.

While it's true that not everything that happens to us is good, it's also true that God can bring good out of everything that happens to us. Romans 8:28 NLT says, "And we know that God causes everything to work together for the good of those who love God and are called according to His purpose for them." That means that even if the devil succeeds in messing up our lives or circumstances somehow, God will bring good out of it in a way that only He can. We can rest assured that just as the Lord has a plan for our lives, He has a plan for every circumstance we'll ever face—and His plans are always to do us good, not harm. (Jer. 29:11.) I believe that it's absolutely essential for us to cooperate with God during our tests and trials. The apostle Paul gives us some insight as to how we can do this when he writes, "I am going to keep on being glad, for I know that as you pray for me, and as the Holy Spirit helps me, this is all going to turn out for my good" (Phil. 1:19 TLB). While there's no substitute for seeking God in prayer on our own behalf, having fellow believers stand in faith with us can be a tremendous asset. If our trials are long and unrelenting, there may be times when it's difficult for us to pray in faith, and those are the times when it greatly

LIVE ON PURPOSE TODAY

Encourage yourself in the Bible today—meditating on Scriptures that speak of your deliverance on its way. And should the Holy Spirit bring someone across your heart who would gladly join you in faith and prayer, call them without delay.

benefits us to have other faith-filled believers interceding for us. Paul goes on to mention the importance of our dependence upon the Holy Spirit for help. If we try to get through our trials in our own wisdom and strength, we will fail miserably. But if we rely on God's guidance and grace, we will position ourselves for the Lord to direct our steps in the paths of victory. Notice how Paul says he's going to "keep on being glad." He knew that he didn't have to wait for his deliverance in order to be joyful. As soon as he began trusting God to bring good out of his situation, he became filled with a sense of hope that produced abundant joy. Over the years, my family and I have witnessed time and time again how God can bring good out of even the most heartbreaking experiences. We've learned that when we put our trust in the Lord and maintain a hopeful attitude in adversity, He can turn our trials into triumphs. No matter what you're going through today, please know that God can supernaturally bring good out of it somehow. And He will do exactly that if you'll adopt an attitude of the heart that declares— "This is all going to turn out for my good!"

PRAYER

Lord, when I'm in the midst of heartbreaking circumstances, help me to turn to You in prayer, and show me who to seek out for prayer support. Teach me to rely on Your Spirit, and to trust You in a way that will enable me to wait for my miracle with joy. Thank You for working all things out for my good and Your glory!

The High Cost
of Complaining

*Do all things without grumbling or disputing; that you may
prove yourselves to be blameless and innocent, children of
God above reproach in the midst of a crooked and perverse
generation, among whom you appear as lights in the world.*

PHILIPPIANS 2:14,15 NASB

A few years ago I heard a well-known minister of the Gospel talking about some of the experiences he and his wife had during their early years of marriage. Even though he is enjoying abundant prosperity now, there was a time when all he and his family could afford was a cold water flat to live in. Times were hard, and he and his wife were tempted to complain about their hardships. But the Holy Spirit gave this godly man a "knowing" that if he wanted the Lord to bless him in extraordinary ways, he and his wife must never grumble about their circumstances. This man and his family were overwhelmed with joy when just a few years later they moved into a beautiful home with stately columns, surrounded by fragrant magnolia trees.

Before I began seriously studying the Bible, I didn't realize how destructive complaining could be. Now I know that it's offensive to God, and it can open the door for Satan to come into our lives to "steal, kill and destroy" (John 10:10). The Old Testament accounts of the Israelites wandering in the desert for 40 years reveal to us that God despised His people's complaints and often judged them for their grumbling. The apostle Paul refers to these accounts when he writes, "Don't grumble as some of them did, for that is why God sent his angel of death to destroy them. All these events happened to them as examples for us. They were written down to warn us..." (1 Cor. 10:10,11 NLT). The truth is that God takes our grumbling personally, and our complaints show a serious lack of gratitude for His boundless mercy and love for us. If you want to cut off the flow of God's blessings in your life, complaining is a good way to do it. On the other hand, being thankful for all He provides for us daily will cause Him to release His abundant blessings into our lives. How would you feel if you gave someone a gift and they responded with indifference, criticism, or complaint? How about if they were overjoyed and overflowing with thankfulness? Their response would naturally determine your treatment of them to a large degree. Should we be surprised if God feels the same way? It's all right to want to make progress and do better in various areas of our lives, but never to the extent that we fail to appreciate and give thanks for the blessings we already have. God expects more from

LIVE ON PURPOSE TODAY

Pay close attention today to the words of your mouth. And if you hear yourself utter anything even close to a grumble, stop yourself in mid sentence. Replace every complaint with a word of praise from a thankful heart.

His children than He does from the rest of the world. That's why He inspired Paul to write, "In everything you do, stay away from complaining and arguing, so that no one can speak a word of blame against you. You are to live clean, innocent lives as children of God in a dark world full of crooked and perverse people. Let your lives shine brightly before them" (Phil. 2:14,15 NLT). It's so natural for us to complain, that when we don't, we stand out—

and people take notice. Do you really want to grab the attention of those people around you who desperately need the Lord in their lives? Refuse to complain or grumble when you're most tempted to. God promises that you'll make an impact on others when you obey Him in this area. The next time you've got the perfect opportunity to let loose with a few complaints, remember what it can cost you. Instead, let a grateful God reward you for resisting the urge to grumble!

PRAYER

Lord, forgive me for all the times I opened my mouth to grumble, instead of to give thanks. Give me a grateful heart, and teach me how to resist the urge to complain. When I obey You in this area, use my example to inspire others and draw them to You. Thank You for my present blessings, and for all those yet to come!

When We Have To Disappoint Others

Seek [God's] will in all you do, and He will direct your paths.

PROVERBS 3:6 NLT

It was one of those days when I wished I could be in two places at the same time. My older son was performing at a music festival to benefit a local Christian coffeehouse, and I wanted to be there for him. It was also a perfect day to visit my mother, who has lived alone since my father died. A visit to her involves almost three hours of traveling time on the road, so I don't get to see her as much as I'd like. Several weeks had already passed since our last visit together. For days I had been praying and seeking the Lord about where He wanted me to be that day. I finally decided to go see my mom, knowing that my son would be terribly disappointed. Hearing the disappointment in my son's voice, I began to feel "torn." This feeling was so real and overwhelming that I actually got out my dictionary and looked up the word *tear* (present tense of *torn*) to see how it would be defined. I found phrases like "a pulling apart by force," "to wound by tearing," and "to force apart or divide into fractions; disrupt; split"[2] That's exactly how I felt.

The fact is that we can't be in two places at the same time, so there will be times when we have to make tough choices. Many times we won't be able to avoid disappointing people—even people who are very special to us. But I believe that if we'll seek God, as the Scripture above advises us, we will be in the right place at the right time, and we can leave the consequences to Him. When I chose to visit my mother, I asked the Lord to speak to my son's heart and help him understand my decision. If we allow guilt and condemnation to torment us every time we choose to be with one person over another, we aren't going to be much good to the person we're with. In addition, the Lord's not likely to honor us for taking the time to "be there" for someone if we don't do it with a right attitude. After I heard the disappointment in my son's voice, I was tempted to resent my mother. I immediately resisted those feelings and prayed for God's grace.

What about when we're the ones being disappointed because others aren't "there" for us? While it's all right for us to share our feelings of disappointment with those who let us down, it's not right for us to indulge in self-pity or hold grudges against them. It's wiser for us to take our disappointment and grievances to God, and ask Him to give us the comfort and consolation we need. If it's a case of someone close to us continually disappointing us, it may be right for us to ask God to change their hearts and help them be more considerate and attentive.

LIVE ON PURPOSE TODAY

Continue thanking God today—and every day—that you're always in the right place at the right time! As those words are ever on your lips, you'll find that your feet are sure to follow.

Today, my prayer for you is that you'll begin seeking the Lord each day and asking Him, "Lord, where do You want me to be?" If you do, you can be sure He'll direct your steps in the paths of His greatest blessings!

PRAYER

Lord, help me to seek Your will for each day so that You'll direct my steps as You've promised. When others are disappointed as a result, I ask that You comfort them and give them understanding. When I'm the one being disappointed, encourage my heart and help me to respond the way You want me to. Thank You that as long as I seek You, I'll always be in the right place at the right time!

The Doubt That Destroys

Above all, you must understand that no prophecy of Scripture came about by the prophet's own interpretation. For prophecy never had its origin in the will of man, but men spoke from God as they were carried along by the Holy Spirit.

2 PETER 1:20,21

When my son John was in high school, he had a friend named Jim whose parents were missionaries. This couple had spent most of their married lives spreading the Gospel and ministering to others. They had raised four wonderful children who were devoted to the Lord. They seemed like the perfect family, and I had great respect and admiration for them. Because of that, I was stunned when I heard that Jim's mother had deserted her husband and children, and eventually moved in with another man. This woman not only turned her back on her family, but on God as well. She wanted nothing to do with Christians or the Bible in her "new life." As a result, her entire family began to fall apart at the seams. Though Jim's father tried desperately to reconcile with his wife, all of his attempts failed, and she eventually divorced him. In an effort to console himself, he hastily entered a second marriage, which turned out to be disastrous. All of the children's lives were devastated by the growing turmoil, and Jim ended up in jail for numerous offenses. I had never witnessed such a good family go so wrong so quickly. When I began earnestly seeking God about it, I believe He revealed to me one of the main causes of the disintegration of this family. The Lord reminded me about a discussion that my husband and Jim's mother had about the Bible when we first met her. She had voiced having serious doubts about the veracity of the Scriptures—saying that "after all, they were written by men"—and I distinctly remember a holy fear coming over me when my husband told me about it.

When Jim's mother began doubting the truth of God's Word, she opened the door for Satan to come into her family and "steal, kill and destroy" (John 10:10). I know from experience that when we don't take God at His Word, we become open to all kinds of wrong philosophies—those belonging to the world and Satan. In Colossians 2:8 NLT, the apostle Paul warns, "Don't let anyone lead you astray with empty philosophy and high-sounding nonsense that come from human thinking and from the evil powers of this world, and not from Christ." Having a working knowledge of God's Word is extremely valuable. But what's just as important is for us to *believe* it. Hebrews 4:2 says that when we don't believe the Word of God, it will have "no value" to us. It's up to us to choose to believe it. When we do, the Lord promises to make it effectual for us so we can walk in victory in every area of our lives. First Thessalonians 2:13 AMP says, "When you received the message of God [which you heard from us], you welcomed it not as the word of [mere] men, but as it truly is, the Word of God, which is effectually at work in you who believe [exercising its superhuman power in those who adhere to and trust in and rely on it]." When Jim's mother began to think of God's Word as written by mere men, she robbed it of its power for her life, and she gave Satan the foothold he needed to rob her of God's protection and

LIVE ON PURPOSE TODAY

As you pray this prayer, allow the joy of the Holy Spirit to flood your heart and mind and bring renewed confidence that God's Word is true. Joy will overtake your doubts.

provision. When I first began studying the Bible about eight years ago, I saw it as the very Word of the living God, and I had more joy and peace in my life than ever before. But after a few years, doubt and unbelief began creeping in and I began suffering from depression, anxiety, and despair. I asked the Lord what had changed, and He led me to a book by a famous Christian author which said that when we begin to doubt God's Word, we open the door for the enemy to come in and invade our minds with destructive thoughts and attitudes. Once I took my stand against all doubt and unbelief, my depression lifted and I regained my peace and joy. One of the most valuable aspects about taking God at His Word is that it gives us stability. Paul talks about this in Ephesians 5:14-15 NLT when he writes, "We will no longer be like children, forever changing our minds about what we believe because someone has told us something different or because someone has cleverly lied to us and made the lie sound like the truth. Instead we will hold to the truth in love, becoming more and more in every way like Christ." Satan is constantly looking for ways he can cause us to doubt God's Word because he knows that if he can succeed, he can get us to believe his lies. Once he accomplishes this, he can virtually control our lives and rob us of the good things God has in store for us. James wrote, "A doubtful mind is as unsettled as a wave of the sea that is driven and tossed by the wind. People like that should not expect to receive anything from the Lord" (James 1:6-8 NLT). My prayer for you today is that you'll take God at His Word and receive all the marvelous blessings He has for you!

PRAYER

Lord, today I ask You to give me a renewed and steadfast faith in Your Word. When I'm tempted to doubt, remind me that my unbelief can cost me a lot more than I'm willing to pay. Thank You that my faith in Your Word will bring me peace, joy, and stability! (Rom. 15:13 NASB.)

Mistakes—
A New Perspective

This is what the Lord says: When people fall down, don't they get up again? When they start down the wrong road and discover their mistake, don't they turn back?

JEREMIAH 8:4 NLT

A few months ago our female pet duck, Daisy, began laying eggs. Since we don't have a farm, my husband, Joe, and I knew that it would be unwise to let Daisy hatch a bunch of ducklings. So we decided to begin taking away her eggs as soon as she laid them. After doing this for many weeks, without seeing Daisy's production slow down one bit, we spoke to our neighbor about the problem, and he suggested that we begin leaving her eggs in her nest. He told us that he grew up on a farm, and that this was the method his family used to stop their ducks from laying. All this time I was seeking the Lord in prayer, asking Him to guide us and to help us do what was wise and pleasing in His sight. My husband and I decided to take our neighbor's advice, and we began leaving Daisy's eggs in her nest. It turned out to be a big mistake. After several weeks, Daisy had laid dozens of eggs, and she began sitting on them to hatch them. After turning to the Lord for more guidance and help, Joe and I decided to take Daisy's eggs from her nest. As difficult as that would be for her, it would be much kinder than letting her have her ducklings, and then giving them away. As I listened to Daisy's cries as she searched in vain for her lost eggs, my heart broke, and all I kept thinking was, *If only I hadn't listened to my neighbor!*

As I shared my regrets and sorrow over my mistakes with my son's wife, Miriam, she said something to me that gave me great comfort and hope. She said that sometimes we have to try the wrong thing before we can know for certain what the right thing is. That really spoke to my heart, and I knew that she was right. I've always said that after we've sought the Lord in prayer for His wisdom and guidance, sooner or later we need to "step out and find out" what His will for us is. There is certainly great value in waiting upon God for specific direction in a matter. But I have found that many times we won't be able to have "all our ducks in a row" before the Lord expects us to make a move. I've been a parent for more than 23 years now. There have been many times when I didn't discover the proper way to deal with my children until I first made some mistakes. Even when I earnestly sought the Lord for His direction, He allowed me to make some mistakes—even serious ones—before I found the right way to deal with certain situations as a parent. The same is true of some of the health problems I've had in the past. There have been times when I didn't discover the proper remedies for my ailments until I tried the wrong ones. It can be especially frustrating when we feel like we've done our best to hear from God, and we still make costly errors. What can we do in cases like these? We can resist

LIVE ON PURPOSE TODAY

Leaving the past behind, but benefiting from valuable hindsight, purpose to "step out and find out" the plans God has in store for you.

feeling sorry for ourselves or assigning blame, and we can refuse to give up hope. We can turn to the Lord yet again, and ask Him to use our mistakes to give us a new and more accurate sense of direction. I've seen Him do this time after time, even in situations that I feared were hopeless. I'm happy to report that Daisy is back to her old self again. And my husband and I now know what *not* to do to try to keep her egg laying under control. My prayer for you today is that you won't allow your fear of making mistakes to keep you from stepping out in faith when God leads you to. Instead, seek the Lord with all your heart, trusting that He will use your wrongs to give you a new and clearer perspective of what's *right!*

PRAYER

Lord, teach me how to turn to You daily for wisdom and guidance in everything. Strengthen my faith so that I won't be so afraid of making mistakes that I'll fail to step out at Your direction. When I do make a mistake, use it to give me a clearer view of what's right. Thank You for making all my crooked paths straight and all my rough ways smooth! (Luke 3:5.)

Exceedingly Abundantly

Now to Him who is able to do exceedingly abundantly above all that we ask or think, according to the power that works in us, to Him be glory....

EPHESIANS 3:20 NKJV

There's a farm about a mile from my house that has a pond with ducks and geese. Passing that pond makes me smile now, but there was a time when it would cause my heart to ache. A pet that my family and I had dearly loved, our female duck Daisy, had died, leaving a void in our hearts and in our little flock that we longed to fill. For five months we went by that pond on a regular basis, watching the ducks at play and looking longingly at the ones that reminded us of our Daisy. At times we even entertained the notion of approaching the owner of the farm and asking him if he'd be willing to part with one of his ducks. Never had we dared to dream how God would exceed our highest expectations in sending us a new pet to love.

After we lost Daisy, we put the word out to all of our duck-related contacts that we were looking to adopt a female duck in need of a good home. Our males, Larry and Ginger, were almost two years old, so we told everyone that we needed a female that was full-grown. She couldn't be too small, because our boys were domestic-sized, and a small duck like a mallard would never survive. The trouble was that large domestic ducks weren't that common in the wild, so this requirement alone was enough to discourage us at times. We felt that it was essential for our boys to accept our new addition, so we told everyone that we would only take a new female on a trial basis. Needless to say, this made our search an even greater challenge. We had tried to get Larry and Ginger to accept females other than Daisy on numerous occasions in the past, and never once were they receptive to the idea. In fact, they were downright hostile. Lastly, my family and I earnestly wanted a new female that was relatively tame, like our boys. We had raised Larry, Ginger, and Daisy almost from birth, and they grew up being held and hugged. As a result, they were much tamer and more people-friendly than their counterparts in the wild. So we told our contacts that we wanted a new pet that wasn't too skittish around people.

All this time, we were lifting our petitions up to the Lord daily. We knew we were asking Him for a lot, but we also knew His promise in Ephesians 3:20 TLB, which says, "Now glory be to God who by his mighty power at work within us is able to do far more than we would ever dare to ask or even dream of—infinitely beyond our highest prayers, desires, thoughts, or hopes." So we got into agreement with God, His Word, and His will for us, and by faith, we positioned ourselves to receive His best in the matter. One day we got a call from a lady who worked for a bird rescue facility about an hour away from our home. She knew about our search, and she said that she was in touch with a family who had rescued a female duck but couldn't keep her. She wasn't at all certain that this duck, which had been

LIVE ON PURPOSE TODAY

Today, be sure that you are in agreement with God—His Word and His will—so that by faith you are positioned for His best.

named Katie, was the pet we were looking for, but she said that we could take her on a trial basis, so we agreed. Upon Katie's arrival, the first thing that struck us was that she was the absolute perfect size for our boys, and that she was strikingly beautiful, unlike any other duck we'd ever seen. The second thing we noticed was that instead of Larry and Ginger being hostile toward her, they were afraid of her! But by the end of the day, all three were getting along so well that we knew they were destined to be the best of friends. Best of all, that very evening, my family and I were able to hold Katie in our arms and hug her. To this day, we call her our "miracle duck," because she has exceeded our highest expectations in every way.

Let me encourage you to pray with a greater level of expectation from now on. God wants to do more in you, through you, and for you than you could ever imagine. And He'll do exactly that if you'll live your life for Him and cooperate with His plans for you. Let me leave you with this precious promise from the Lord today: "God can do anything, you know—far more than you could ever imagine or guess or request in your wildest dreams!" (Eph. 3:20 MESSAGE).

PRAYER

Lord, please forgive me for the times I've prayed with little faith or expectation. Give me a growing passion for Your presence and Your Word so that my faith in You will grow in leaps and bounds. Teach me to take my needs and desires straight to You, and help me to pray bold prayers that will get results that exceed my highest expectations in every way. Thank You that as I follow Your lead, You'll do things on my behalf far above my wildest dreams!

Prophesying Our Future

You will also declare a thing and it will be established for you.

JOB 22:28 NKJV

Some years ago, a relative of mine was involved in an incident that threatened to land him in prison. While we waited for the legal process to be accomplished, I went around telling people that if my loved one had to go to jail, I would have a nervous breakdown. I made the statement half-jokingly, but part of me really believed it. As it turned out, my relative *was* sentenced to prison, and within a year's time, my mental health broke down to the point where I needed tranquilizers, anti-depressants, and psychiatric care just to cope.

The Lord brought this incident to my remembrance recently to highlight the impact my words can have on my own future. I was not a committed Christian at the time, and I had no working knowledge of the Bible. No one had ever told me that my words have authority in this earthly realm, and that the words I speak over myself can have awesome consequences. Proverbs 18:21 AMP says, "Death and life are in the power of the tongue, and they who indulge in it shall eat the fruit of it [for death or life]." I've heard some preaching that warns that we can literally prophesy our own futures to some extent. I've also learned that some well-respected ministers of the Gospel believe that Mark 11:23 can be taken in a negative sense, as well as a positive one. In this verse, Jesus says that whoever "believes that those things he says will come to pass, he will have whatever he says." What if it *is* true that this principle can work in a negative sense? If so, then I shouldn't wonder why I actually did have mental health problems after voicing that I expected to have them. Job 22:28 NKJV says, "You will also declare a thing and it will be established for you." Verses like these have given me a holy fear concerning the words I speak over my life and the lives of others.

Sometimes I can't help wondering how I might have reacted to this same incident if it occurred after I became devoted to the Lord and His Word. I'd like to think that I might have had an attitude that said, "Yes, this will be hard to deal with at first, but God has promised to stick with me through the difficult times, and He will see me through it." I know now that when we and others speak negative things over our lives, they are not from God, but from our own fleshly attitudes or from Satan himself. And in these cases, Jeremiah 23:16 NKJV would apply: "They speak a vision of their own heart, not from the mouth of the Lord." I know this without a doubt because God says, "I know the plans I have for you; plans to prosper you and not to harm you, plans to give you hope and a future" (Jer. 29:11).

LIVE ON PURPOSE TODAY

Ask the Holy Spirit to help you guard your mouth and speak words of life. Begin to listen as you speak, and if you hear yourself speaking negative words—*stop!* Repent! And align the words of your mouth with God's Words that always produce abundant life.

When negative circumstances threaten to enter our lives, we don't have to expect to fall apart or to experience dark times. We don't have to anticipate being left without hope. We can cling to our

God and His precious promises of supernatural assistance in our times of need. And we can confidently declare with the psalmist, "God is our refuge and strength, an ever-present help in trouble. Therefore, we will not fear, though the earth give way and the mountains fall into the heart of the sea…" (Ps. 46:1,2).

PRAYER

Lord, give me a keen awareness and a holy fear of how my words and attitudes can impact my future. Teach me how to speak words of life and hope over my own life and those of others. When troubles threaten to overwhelm me, remind me that with You by my side, I never need to expect to fall or fail. Thank You for planning a future filled with hope and good things for me!

Dependence Vs. Independence

Without Me, you can do nothing.

JOHN 15:5 NKJV

These words spoken by Jesus radically changed my life. I had grown up hearing that old saying, "God helps those who help themselves," so I believed that God wanted us to be independent and self-reliant. Then I discovered that, not only is this phrase not in the Bible, but it contradicts the principles of Scripture. Hebrews 11:6 TLB says, "You can never please God without faith, without depending on him." The truth is that God is pleased when we rely on Him and seek His help. Psalm 37:5 TLB says, "Commit everything you do to the Lord. Trust him to help you do it and he will." God wants to be partners with us in all our daily tasks and activities. When we invite God on the scene, an unlimited amount of resources and possibilities are made available to us. It's an "I can't, but God can" kind of lifestyle. And with God, there is no matter that concerns us which is too small or insignificant; there is no distinction between sacred and secular. God wants to be involved in every aspect of our lives, and He wants to help us reach our God-given potential. He also wants to ease our burdens and struggles. Psalm 34:5 NLT says, "Those who look to Him for help will be radiant with joy." Depending on God brings joy, peace, and satisfaction. But trying to accomplish things on our own makes us weary, frustrated, and discouraged. That's exactly why Satan wants us to think we don't need to ask God for help. He knows that the more we depend on God, the more productive and successful we'll be.

The apostle Paul said, "I can do all things through Christ who strengthens me" (Phil. 4:13 NKJV). Paul knew that his strength came from his dependence upon and union with Christ. Ours does, too. Asking God for help doesn't make us weak—it makes us strong. What really makes us weak is trying to do things on our own, in our own strength. Just try to be a parent, spouse, or student without God's help, and you will end up drained and defeated. But if you seek the Lord daily and depend on Him, He will sustain you and lead you to victory, no matter what challenges come your way. In 2 Corinthians 12:9 NLT, the Lord told Paul, "My power works best in your weakness." When we acknowledge our weaknesses and ask for God's help, it gives Him the opportunity to show what an awesome difference His involvement can make. It delights the heart of God when we say, "Lord, without You, I can do nothing. Please help me." Often I hear myself praying like this many times a day, especially when I'm tackling tough situations and tasks. As a result, I've always discovered a newfound strength, peace, and confidence that enabled me to persevere and complete the task with joy. It's my prayer that you'll begin depending on God more each day, so that you can join your praises with the psalmist who wrote, "Great is the Lord, who enjoys helping his servant"! (Ps. 60:12 NLT).

LIVE ON PURPOSE TODAY

Prayerfully decide today which tasks you've been trying to handle on your own that could be handled much better with God's help. Hand them over to the Master!

PRAYER

Lord, forgive me for failing to invite You to be a part of my daily endeavors. When I try to do things in my own strength, remind me to ask for Your help. Deliver me from an independent spirit, and enable me to depend on You more and more. Thank You for the peace, joy, and success that will be mine!

Believe and See His Glory

Against all hope, Abraham in hope believed and so became the father of many nations, just as it had been said to him, "So shall your offspring be." Without weakening in his faith, he faced the fact that his body was as good as dead—since he was about a hundred years old—and that Sarah's womb was also dead. Yet he did not waver through unbelief regarding the promise of God, but was strengthened in his faith and gave glory to God, being fully persuaded that God had power to do what he had promised.

ROMANS 4:18-21

These verses are a great encouragement to those of us who have ever had to endure long periods of waiting before we saw the fulfillment of God's promises to us. The emphasis here is upon the fact that Abraham's situation was completely hopeless. Yet, he believed God's promise to give him a son in his old age. It was many years before God fulfilled this promise to Abraham, and he made some mistakes during those years. Still, these verses don't mention Abraham's doubts, but focus instead on his faith. That fact should encourage us, too. Though we may struggle with our own doubts from time to time, if we hold on to God's promises, we will receive our reward just as Abraham did.

If you are not feeling very hopeful today that God's promises to you will ever come to pass, I urge you to hold on to your faith. Look at these verses in Hebrews 10:35-36 NLT: "Do not throw away this confident trust in the Lord, no matter what happens. Remember the great reward it brings you! Patient endurance is what you need now, so you will continue to do God's will. Then you will receive all that He has promised." If you throw your faith

LIVE ON PURPOSE TODAY

Whether you feel like it or not, whether your faith is on the brink of faltering or you are standing strong, lift your hands even now and offer thanksgiving and praise to the One who always keeps His promise of victory to those who trust Him.

away before God fulfills His promises to you, you will never receive the reward He has waiting for you. Ask the Lord to give you the patience and endurance you need to stand strong, then do your part by hanging in there when the going gets tough. Hebrews 6:12 TLB says, "Be anxious to follow the example of those who receive all that God has promised them because of their strong faith and patience." Follow Abraham's example and receive all that the Lord has promised you. Not only will you be blessed, but God will be glorified through you, and then you can be an example to someone else whose faith is faltering. The Living Bible says that Abraham "praised God for this blessing even before it happened." If you'll begin thanking God right now for the fulfillment of those promises that look like they'll never come to pass, your faith will grow in leaps and bounds and you will delight the heart of God. Take heart from this precious verse in 2 Timothy 2:13 TLB: "Even when we are too weak to have any faith left, he remains faithful to us and will help us, for he cannot disown us who are part of himself, and he will always carry out his promises to us"!

PRAYER

Lord, whenever I'm tempted to doubt Your promises, increase my faith and give me the patience I need to stand strong. Help me to take my eyes off my circumstances and rest them on Your promises. Thank You for enabling me to receive all that You have promised!

Christlike Compassion

Being happy-go-lucky around a person whose heart is heavy is as bad as stealing his jacket in cold weather, or rubbing salt in his wounds.

PROVERBS 25:20 TLB

Recently, my husband's company had a round of layoffs that lasted for several months. During this time, there was an executive in the company that took it upon herself to "coach" those who were told that they were being let go. Instead of showing these people the compassion they desperately needed, she made light of their situation and tried to get them to look at the "bright side." When this executive became a victim of layoffs herself, she shocked everyone by becoming sour and spiteful, and willfully damaging company property before her departure.

I believe that one of the biggest mistakes that we Christians make is failing to respond to others with Christlike compassion when they are going through difficult times. I must confess that I have been guilty of this offense myself. In an effort to cheer someone up or give them hope, I've said things like—"Pray harder," or "Spend more time reading the Bible." The truth of the matter is that sometimes the best thing we can do for someone who's going through a trial is to just listen with a compassionate ear or cry along with them. Scripture says, "Rejoice with those who rejoice, and weep with those who weep" (Rom. 12:15 NASB). The New Living Translation puts it this way: "When others are happy, be happy with them. If they are sad, share their sorrow." In other words, God wants us to genuinely empathize and sympathize with others when they are hurting. The best rule of thumb in situations like these may be one that Jesus gave us in Luke 6:31 TLB: "Treat others as you want them to treat you." When we're suffering, the last thing we want is someone minimizing or shrugging off our problems. Proverbs 25:20 TLB says, "Being happy-go-lucky around a person whose heart is heavy is as bad as stealing his jacket in cold weather, or rubbing salt in his wounds." While we don't want to encourage a hurting person to indulge in self-pity or drown in despair, we also don't want to "rub salt in their wounds" by making light of their pain or ignoring it altogether.

I've heard some well-respected ministers say that one of the main reasons the Lord allows us to experience trials is so that we can be more compassionate and understanding toward others in their own times of adversity. I believe that's true. When someone we know is going through a negative experience that we've been through ourselves, we have the unique privilege of being able to say to them, "I know how you feel, and I understand." When I was having major troubles with my son during his teenage years, I was most encouraged and comforted by other parents who had endured similar problems with their own teens. Even though these folks couldn't offer me any concrete solutions, just hearing them say something like, "I've been there, and I feel your pain," made all the difference.

LIVE ON PURPOSE TODAY

Do you know someone today who is hurting? Find a way to express love to them and demonstrate true Christlike compassion.

If that woman executive at my husband's company had first-hand knowledge of what it was like to be suddenly jobless *before* she attempted to counsel her laid-off coworkers, she might have reacted differently to their sad news. Instead, all she did was expose her hypocrisy and lose the respect of those around her. The apostle Paul warned us against this kind of hypocrisy when he wrote, "You, therefore, have no excuse, you who pass judgment on someone else, for at whatever point you judge the other, you are condemning yourself, because you who pass judgment do the same things" (Rom. 2:1). Paul goes on to state: "You then, who teach others, do you not teach yourself?" (Rom. 2:21). In order for us to make an impact on the world—to be the salt and light Jesus calls us to be—we've got to be "real" and not phonies. With God's help, we can reach out to hurting people with the compassion of Christ, and we can set a Christlike example for others when we are the ones who are hurting. Let's let the world see our compassion. Let's let them see our joy in the midst of trouble. Let's let them see Jesus in us!

PRAYER

Lord Jesus, You said, "You must be compassionate, just as your Father is compassionate" (Luke 6:36 NLT). So I ask You to help me to "put on a heart of compassion," each day, just as Your Word instructs (Col. 3:12 NASB). Guard me from indifference, coldness, and bitterness, and keep me free from hypocrisy. Thank You that as I seek to follow You daily, You will touch and change lives through me!

My Father Is Greater Than All

My Father, who has given them to Me, is greater than all.

JOHN 10:29

Recently, when I was going through a very difficult time and earnestly seeking the Lord, He brought it to my attention that I was focusing entirely too much on the devil and not enough on God. As a result, I was feeling more and more fearful, depressed, and hopeless. The Lord led me to the Scripture above, and He impressed upon me to meditate on the phrase, "My Father is greater than all." Every time negative feelings threatened to overwhelm me, I reminded myself of this powerful truth, and I could sense a calmness crowding out my fears.

I often hear from people who say something like, "The devil is really doing a number on me!" I can sympathize with them because I know those feelings all too well myself. The good news is that if we will make the effort to remind ourselves of some powerful truths from God's Word, we can be the overcomers that the Lord wants us to be. First of all, we need to remember that only God is all-powerful. Also, God limits the activities of Satan and his demonic forces. And to some extent, we can, too. James 4:7 says, "Submit yourselves to God. Resist the devil, and he will flee from you." By sinning, we can give Satan the opportunity to come into our lives to "steal, kill and destroy" (John 10:10). But by living in submission to God's will and resisting temptation when it comes, we can slam the door in the devil's face and severely limit his involvement in our lives.

Another way we can hinder Satan's activities against us is to "pray without ceasing," like the Bible says (1 Thess. 5:17 KJV). For those of us who belong to the Lord, prayer should be like breathing. We are in a continuous battle with the forces of evil, and by keeping in constant communication with our divine Commander-in-Chief and relying on His power and guidance, we can avoid a lot of the traps and obstacles that the enemy puts in our way. As we give God first place in our lives, and as we trust and obey Him in every situation, we can count on Him to fight our battles for us so that we can live the life of rest and peace that He's called us to. (Heb. 4:3; Col. 3:15.)

If you have put your hope in Christ, then you have been equipped with heavenly weapons to be an overcomer. I urge you to make a commitment to dig into God's Word and discover for yourself how the Lord has provided you with everything you need to walk in victory. The apostle John reminds us that because we have been born of God, the One who lives in us (God) is greater than the one who is in the world (Satan). (1 John 4:4.) And Paul reminds us that the Lord is not neutral when he writes, "If God is for us, who can be against us?" (Rom. 8:31). On our own, we can do nothing. (John 15:5.) But with God on our side, "we are more than conquerors" (Rom. 8:37).

LIVE ON PURPOSE TODAY

Over and over repeat the phrase from John 10:29 out loud to yourself: "My Father is greater than all." These six powerful words of Scripture will build faith on the inside of you sufficient to uproot defeat and usher in victory.

It's true that Satan is a formidable opponent. But he's no match for God. When we fear the devil and concentrate on his activities, we actually play into his hands and give him the kind of attention and control he thrives on. But when we keep our eyes on God and attend to His Word, we strengthen our defenses against satanic attack. The next time you are in a trial and are feeling "under attack," make a conscious decision not to focus on the devil's destructiveness, but on God's greatness. Take heart and remember the Savior's words—your Father is greater than all!

PRAYER

Lord, help me to focus on Your greatness and goodness when I'm going through difficult times. When I'm tempted to fear the devil and his activities, remind me that as long as I fear and reverence You alone, I need fear nothing else. (Isa. 8:13,14.) Teach me how to encourage myself with the truth of Your Word so that I'll have a keen awareness of who I am in Christ and who You are to me. Thank You for fighting my battles and enabling me to live a life of victory and rest!

Benefit Yourself

If you give, you will get! Your gift will return to you in full and overflowing measure, pressed down, shaken together to make room for more, and running over. Whatever measure you use to give—large or small— will be used to measure what is given back to you.

LUKE 6:38 TLB

Before I was married, while I was still living at home with my parents, my father had a rule that said that as long as my sisters and I were in school, we wouldn't have to pay him room and board. I never liked this rule, especially since I suspected it was just one of my dad's ploys to get his kids to go to college. After I graduated from high school I did begin attending a local college. During my second year there, I met my husband in one of my classes. Soon afterward we began making wedding plans, and I decided to quit school and go to work full-time. I reluctantly began paying my father the required room and board each week, which I felt was too much, especially since I needed the money more than he did. As my wedding got closer—and as my resentment grew—I began missing more and more of my payments to my dad. But he never said a word. He and my mom gave my husband and me a lavish wedding and showered us with extravagant gifts. Several years later, after the birth of our second child, my father presented my husband and me with a sizable cash gift to buy a much-needed car. I was speechless and I felt ashamed when he told me that, included in the gift, was all the money I had paid him each week before I got married. To this day I marvel at my father's kindness and generosity, as well as his forgiving nature. He knew that I resented giving him that money each week, and that I gave it grudgingly. But he never held it against me and he gave it all back to me—and more.

When I disobeyed my dad and neglected to give him all that he asked for, I hurt myself more than anyone else. God used this experience to show me that when He demands something from us, it's ultimately for our own good. Jesus said, "Blessed are the merciful, for they will be shown mercy" (Matt. 5:7). He also said, "Forgive, and you will be forgiven" (Luke 6:37). When we choose to be merciful and forgive those who hurt us, we are positioning ourselves to receive mercy and forgiveness from the Lord and others when we need it most. Each time we decide to let go of our anger, bitterness, and resentment, we are rewarded with a peace, joy, and freedom that we could never have otherwise. Jesus said, "Just as you want people to treat you, treat them the same way" (Luke 6:31 NASB). One reason He gives us this command is because He knows that whenever we mistreat people, it will eventually come back to haunt us. When God commands us to give generously out of our finances, it's not because He needs the money. It's because He wants us to be partners with Him in doing His work and advancing His kingdom on this earth. And it's just another way for God to bless us. Jesus said, "Give and it will be

LIVE ON PURPOSE TODAY

Ask the Lord to lead you to someone today that He desires for you to bless with finances, time, a task, or even a simple expression of love. Go quickly and sow generously!

given to you" (Luke 6:38). And in Philippians 4:17, the apostle Paul talks about how our giving to others will be "credited to our account." We need to have the attitude about our possessions that David did when he said to the Lord, "Everything comes from You, and we have given You only what comes from Your hand" (Chron. 29:14). Even giving others the gift of encouragement can benefit us, according to Proverbs 11:25: "He who refreshes others will himself be refreshed." Each time we lift someone up with a kind word or deed, we are paving the way for God to ensure that others will be there for us when we're the ones in need of a lift. The bottom line is this: God's not trying to take anything away from us—He's trying to give to us and bless us. He's not trying to make life more difficult for us—He's trying to make it easier and more abundant. I pray that today you'll get ahold of these life-changing truths and put them in operation to discover for yourself that "the merciful, kind, and generous man benefits himself—for his deeds return to bless him"! (Prov. 11:17 AMP).

PRAYER

*Lord, remind me that I'm going to reap
what I sow in this life. (Gal. 6:7.)
Give me an understanding of how I forfeit blessings
when I don't do things Your way. Help me to sow seeds
of mercy, kindness, and forgiveness wherever I go.
Thank You that as I sow generously—blessing others, I will
reap generously—and with blessings! (2 Cor. 9:6 AMP.)*

Individual Ministry Needs

Your godly lives will speak to them better than any words.

1 PETER 3:2 TLB

Recently, I was talking to a relative of mine about how one of my sisters, who had always been disinterested in the things of God, had begun asking my advice about seeking the Lord. When I began to relate how God had already begun working wonders on her behalf, my relative exclaimed, "But she doesn't even go to church!" I had expected him to rejoice in my sister's decision to turn to the Lord and that God was already pouring out His blessings upon her, but instead he became indignant.

Would it shock you if I said that I believe that Christians who don't go to church can still get to heaven? I'm not the only one who thinks this way. So do many of the most well-respected ministers of the Gospel. I'm not bringing this up to discourage people from going to church. I believe that it's God's will for Christians to attend church regularly, and we are most likely out of His will when we don't. But I must confess that I am troubled by believers who think that the lost can only be saved by going to church. I often hear from believers who ask me to pray that someone they've been trying to minister to would go to church with them, and I'm always happy to do so. There's no question that many lost people have been saved through churches throughout the ages. But what about the people who may never see the inside of a church? I once heard a godly man say, "You may be the only Bible that someone ever reads." Some Christians don't want to hear this, because it puts too much responsibility on them. They would much rather talk an unbeliever into attending church with them, than to live their lives as "living epistles read of all men," so that lives might be changed through their Christlike behavior (2 Cor. 3:2,3). But where does that leave the folks who will never be persuaded to go to church?

I have another relative who hasn't attended church since he was very young. He was brought up in the church, but drifted away as he got older and struck out on his own. Now that he is approaching middle age, he realizes how empty he feels inside and how much something is missing in his life. When he visited me recently, he confessed that he had been reading my devotionals online for more than a year, and he had developed a growing hunger to have a personal relationship with the Lord. But he was hesitant to tell anyone about it, because he was afraid that they would only try to drag him to church. He had tried that route more than once, and each time he was completely turned off to the things of God, even though he attended churches that had entirely different styles of worship. He asked me many questions about the Lord and my relationship with Him, and I gave him one of my study Bibles. He was deeply touched and promised to read it, and to let me know how he was doing. I told him that I would be praying for him and that he could contact me anytime if he needed prayer or had any more questions. He has kept in touch with me,

LIVE ON PURPOSE TODAY

Be ever conscious that every day in every way you are a living epistle read of all men. "Your godly lives will speak to them better than any words" (1 Peter 3:2 TLB).

and he is reading God's Word and praying like never before. He says he feels like he has "a new beginning."

I don't know if my sister will ever attend a church service. But I'm not worried about it, because I have witnessed how she is seeking God with all her heart, and how the Lord is already rewarding her and revealing Himself to her. And who am I to judge her? Instead, I will continue to pray for her and to do my best to encourage her to live her life for God. And I will resist becoming indignant when the Lord blesses her abundantly—even if she doesn't go to church.

PRAYER

Lord, use me to draw others to You and to Your life-changing truth. Help me to see each person as an individual, with very unique and personal needs. Teach me to seek You for wisdom in how to minister effectively to each individual. And remind me that Jesus said, "Stop judging by mere appearances and make a right judgment" (John 7:24). I pray that when I see the lost turning to You—and You blessing them as a result—I will not judge them or presume that I know their hearts. Thank You that as I strive to be more like Jesus each day, You will touch and change lives through me!

Overlooked and Unappreciated

Then the king said to Zadok, 'Take the ark of God back into the city. If I find favor in the Lord's eyes, He will bring me back and let me see it and His dwelling place again. But if He says, 'I am not pleased with you,' then I am ready; let Him do to me whatever seems good to Him.

2 SAMUEL 15:25,26

These words of King David have been a profound inspiration to me at times when I've felt overlooked, passed over, or treated unfairly. David is considered by many to be the most victorious warrior of all time, and yet when his own son, Absalom, conspires against him to steal his throne, instead of retaliating, he commits himself to God and His sense of justice. He doesn't whine, complain, or feel sorry for himself. He just basically says, "Lord, I put myself in Your hands. Do with me whatever You think is right. I trust You." And David's attitude was a Christlike one, according to the Scripture which says, "When [Jesus] suffered, He did not threaten to get even. He left His case in the hands of God, who always judges fairly" (1 Peter 2:23 NLT). As it turned out, the Lord did restore David to his throne, and I believe that his unwavering trust in God was the main reason why.

Sooner or later all of us will experience the pain and disappointment of having our efforts ignored, minimized, or criticized by others. I believe that how we respond in times like these not only indicates our level of spiritual maturity, but also determines our outcome. One thing that helps me is remembering that whatever we do should be done "unto the Lord." The apostle Paul wrote, "Work hard and cheerfully at all you do, just as though you were working for the Lord and not merely for your masters, remembering that it is the Lord Christ who is going to pay you, giving you your full portion of all He owns. He is the one you are really working for" (Col. 3:23,24 TLB). These verses clearly convey the perspective we should have in all we do. If we focus on pleasing God and doing our best in everything, we won't be so resentful, hurt, or discouraged when others don't appreciate or reward our efforts. Instead, we can rest secure in the knowledge that God is fully aware of all we do, and He will see that we get the recognition and reward we deserve in His perfect way and timing. Even if those we are working for are continually unreasonable or unfair, we can take heart from God's reassurance that "nothing can hinder the Lord" (1 Sam. 14:6 NLT). There may be times when it looks like others are succeeding in delaying or preventing our progress, but the truth is that when God decides to bless and promote His people, no person on earth and no devil in hell can stop Him.

LIVE ON PURPOSE TODAY

When you're tempted to feel overlooked and unappreciated, encourage yourself with the Scriptures above. Read them, meditate upon them, and be enlivened by them!

If you can relate to this message today, let me encourage you to get your eyes off other people and get them squarely on God. Work hard and do your best in all you do, trusting that the Lord Himself will honor you for it, even if others don't. Let your declaration of faith be the psalmist's: "You will give me greater honor than before, and turn again and comfort me"! (Ps. 71:22 TLB).

PRAYER

Lord, I believe that true honor and promotion
come from You. (Ps. 75:6,7 TLB.)
When my efforts are overlooked or unappreciated,
I ask that You help me to respond in a Christlike manner.
Strengthen me to resist becoming angry, resentful, frustrated, or
discouraged. Show me how to pray for those who treat me unfairly.
Thank You that as I depend on You for justice and reward, You
will lift me up and exalt me at the proper time! (1 Peter 5:6.)

From Grief to Gladness

*I am going to keep on being glad, for I know that
as you pray for me, and as the Holy Spirit helps me,
this is all going to turn out for my good.*

PHILIPPIANS 1:19 TLB

Recently, I experienced a loss that grieved my heart and sent my emotions into a tailspin. I know that the Bible tells us that it's all right for us to mourn over a loss, and that we will be comforted as a result. (Matt. 5:4.) But I also know that when our grief is prolonged, it can lead to depression and despair. Even those of us who live for God and trust in His Word and promises can become disillusioned pretty quickly when we suffer a loss of some kind. We can even become angry at God and question His intentions. And even though the Bible assures us that the Lord is always with us, we can feel forgotten and forsaken.

After feeling grief-stricken for quite some time, I began to sense the Lord prompting me to begin thanking Him in advance for all the good He was going to bring out of my loss. He reminded me of the apostle Paul, and how when he suffered the most unimaginable trials and heartaches, he declared, "This is all going to turn out for my good!" (Phil. 1:19 TLB). As I began to shift my focus from what I had *lost*—to what I could *gain* from this painful experience, I began to experience the gladness that Paul talks about when he says, "I am going to keep on being glad." I took great comfort in Paul's words, "as the Holy Spirit helps me." And instead of focusing on my own inadequacies, I tried to focus on the awesome power of God's Spirit at work in me. Most of all, I prayed. Each time I felt that sinking feeling starting to pull me down, I asked the Lord to strengthen and comfort me. I also asked others to pray for me. I knew that if a great man of faith like the apostle Paul needed the prayers of others, I certainly did, too. His words, "as you pray for me," reveal his reliance upon intercessory prayer.

Proverbs 15:15 AMP says, "All the days of the desponding and afflicted are made evil [by anxious thoughts and forebodings], but he who has a glad heart has a continual feast [regardless of circumstances]." Paul knew the importance and power of a glad heart, and how it could lift us above our circumstances. He knew that the Bible says, "The joy of the Lord is our strength" (Neh. 8:10). And he was keenly aware that prolonged sadness can weaken us and make us highly vulnerable to satanic attack. Paul wrote, "We are pressed on every side by troubles, but not crushed and broken. We are perplexed because we don't know why things happen as they do, but we don't give up and quit.... We get knocked down, but we get up again and keep going" (2 Cor. 4:8,9 TLB). Not everything that happens to us in this life will be good. But when we put our trust in God and His goodness, He will bring good out of everything that comes our way. (Rom. 8:28.)

LIVE ON PURPOSE TODAY

No matter where you are or what you're doing, if you sense that sinking feeling of grief starting to pull you down, stop and call upon the Lord. Ask Him for strength and comfort, and He'll provide them for you!

During this time I took a nasty fall and suffered a severe knee injury. As I described the pain, swelling, and discoloration of my knee to one of my dearest friends, instead of indulging my per-verse need for self-pity, she tried to make me see the beauty in my bruises. Suddenly, thanks to her positive perspective, I began to see a rainbow on my knee, instead of an ugly wound. If you have suffered a loss or hurt of some kind, I encourage you to shift your focus from what you have lost to what you will gain through your painful experience. You will not only find relief and healing, but the Lord will reward your faith in ways that will bless you and glorify Him. It's my heartfelt prayer that by the power of God's Spirit, you'll be able to declare like Paul, "I am going to keep on being glad!"

PRAYER

Lord, in times of loss or sorrow, remind me that because of my relationship with You, I can still have an inner peace and joy. Help me not to hesitate to ask You to strengthen and comfort me when I begin to feel overwhelmed. Guard me from depression and despair, and help me to do my part in the process. Thank You that as I trust You to bring good out of my pain, You will turn my grief to gladness!

The Power of Forgiveness

*Dear friends, never avenge yourselves. Leave that to God,
for he has said that he will repay those who deserve it. [Don't
take the law into your own hands.] Instead, feed your enemy
if he is hungry. If he is thirsty give him something to drink and
you will be "heaping coals of fire on his head." In other words, he
will feel ashamed of himself for what he has done to you. Don't
let evil get the upper hand but conquer evil by doing good.*

ROMANS 12:19-21 TLB

One day, when my son Joseph was only about six years old, he came home from school without his lunch box. I asked him where it was, and when he said he didn't know, I suggested that he mentally retrace his steps. As my son got more and more confused, I got more and more angry. It seemed like he was always misplacing something, and for me, this was like the last straw. I told him that when he went to school the following day, he had better go to the office and check the "Lost and Found." Over the next few days my son tried everything to find that lunch box but to no avail. I was really disgusted with him, and I made sure that he knew it. Then one evening I opened up one of my kitchen cabinets and was horrified when I discovered the missing lunch box inside. I had packed my son's lunch, and then, instead of handing it to him as he walked out the door, I put it in one of our cabinets. With a heavy heart I approached my son and asked him to forgive me for accusing him of losing his lunch box. Without a moment's hesitation, he threw his little arms around my neck and kissed me and exclaimed, "That's okay, Mommy!" It was a lesson in forgiveness that I've never forgotten.

These days, whenever someone attacks or hurts me, I try to remember how so many years ago, my little boy showed me that being kind and forgiving to those who wound us can cause them to feel the regret and repentance that God wants them to. Jesus has commanded us to forgive our enemies, to pray for them, and to resist treating them as badly as they treat us. (Luke 6:27,28.) Our Lord has called us to live "the most excellent way," by "keeping no record of wrongs" (1 Cor. 12:31; 13:5). And He expects us to do the right thing, even when the right thing is not being done to us. If you have trusted Christ as your Savior, the Spirit of God dwells on the inside of you, and He will empower you to forgive those who offend you the moment you make the decision to forgive. In addition, God has given you the supernatural ability to love others with His kind of love. (Rom. 5:5.) Does God care if we're mistreated? You bet He does. And the Bible makes it clear that He is committed to protecting and defending those who are devoted to Him. But

LIVE ON PURPOSE TODAY

Survey your heart and make sure you hold no grudges toward anyone. If you find even the slightest hint of animosity, make it right! After all, if you don't forgive sins, what are you going to do with them? (John 20:23 MESSAGE.)

He expects us to "leave room for God's wrath" by refusing to avenge ourselves, and giving Him the opportunity to fight for us (Rom. 12:19). The reason why we don't see more believers winning battles is because too often we don't want to wait on God to defend and rescue us. We plunge ahead and try to fight our own battles, and as a result, we forfeit the victories and blessings God had in store for us as a reward for trusting Him. We need to remind ourselves that just because we let someone off the hook for wronging us, that doesn't mean they're off God's hook. When we forgive those who hurt us, we aren't excusing their actions; we're just forgiving them as an act of obedience to God, and we're trusting Him to deal with them. We can't expect our feelings to help us. We have to do it as an act of our will, and we may have to do it by faith. After we make the decision to forgive, often our emotions will fall in line. When Jesus spoke about prayer and mountain-moving faith, He said we had to let go of all unforgiveness in order for God to forgive us our sins. (Mark 11:22-25.) We can't expect our prayers to get ready answers when we are holding grudges. Ephesians 4:32 MESSAGE says, "Be gentle with one another, sensitive. Forgive one another as quickly and thoroughly as God in Christ forgave you." When bitterness begins to take root in our hearts, it can poison us spiritually and make us physically and emotionally sick. (Heb. 12:15.) It can also open the door to satanic attack. (Eph. 4:27.) Let me leave you with some food for thought from the Message Bible today: "If you forgive someone's sins, they're gone for good. If you don't forgive sins, what are you going to do with them?" (John 20:23 MESSAGE).

PRAYER

Lord, help me to be quick to forgive those who treat me unjustly, to respond in a Christlike manner, and to pray for them. Remind me that "I can do everything God asks me to with the help of Christ who gives me the strength and power" (Phil. 4:13 TLB). Thank You that as I sow seeds of mercy, I will reap mercy! (Matt. 5:7.)

The Truth About "Venting"

I grew up in a generation that was taught by mental health
"experts" that it was often helpful to "vent" our anger and
frustration on others. It wasn't until I began seriously studying the Bible that I realized that, though venting was the world's
way of handling negative emotions, it was not God's way. I finally
figured out that this was probably the reason why it usually did
more harm than good, no matter what the so-called experts said.

Though Jesus equates anger with murder in the above
verses, the Bible does not condemn all forms of anger. There is
such a thing as "righteous indignation," the kind of anger that
Jesus demonstrated when he turned over the tables of the money
changers in the temple. (John 2:14-16.) Showing the right kind of
anger can let people know that we are serious, and it can lead us
and others to take constructive action. But this kind of beneficial
anger is more rare than we usually think. Jesus warns us that our
words carry a lot of weight, and we will be accountable to God for
everything we say. In Matthew 12:36-37, Jesus says, "I tell you
that men will have to give account on the day of judgment for
every careless word they have spoken. For by your words you will
be acquitted, and by your words you will be condemned." It's been

said, "You can't un-ring a bell." Once harsh and hurtful words have left our mouths, the consequences for them have been set into motion, and even if we apologize for them later on, the damage has already been done. As the apostle Paul wrote, "Steer clear of foolish discussions which lead people into the sin of anger with each other. Things will be said that will burn and hurt for a long time to come" (2 Tim. 2:16,17 TLB).

The truth is that the principle of venting our anger and frustration is a product of the "Me Generation." It's a way of making ourselves feel better at the expense of another. It's selfishness at its worst, and it's highly destructive to lives and relationships. One thing we need to ask ourselves when we're tempted to vent is, "What are my motives here?" If we're venting just to make ourselves feel better, or to "get even" with someone who we feel has wronged us, then we're most likely out of God's will, and that's sin. The Bible says, "In your anger do not sin: Do not let the sun go down while you are still angry, and do not give the devil a foothold" (Eph. 4:26,27). The New Living Translation translation says, "Don't sin by letting anger gain control over you." As followers of Christ, we are expected to allow the Holy Spirit to control us at all times. (Rom. 8:9.) Once we allow anger to control us, we're acting more like the devil than Jesus. Scripture says, "If anyone considers himself religious and yet does not keep a tight rein on his tongue, he deceives himself and his religion is worthless" (James 1:26).

LIVE ON PURPOSE TODAY

Spend extra time today in God's Word focusing on Scriptures that boost your love walk. Then find someone to love!

Here's the bottom line: If we have given our life to God, we no longer have the right to vent our negative emotions the way the world does.

Yes, there are times when God expects us to confront others about their wrong behavior. But the Lord expects us to seek His wisdom and guidance as to when and how that should be. And our attitudes and motives must be right. Galatians 6:1 says, "If someone is caught in a sin, you who are spiritual should restore him gently. But watch yourself, or you also may be tempted." This kind of confrontation and correction seeks restoration, rather than ruin. And it is done with a spirit of humility, rather than pride. What the mental health experts never told us was that when others hurt us, we could take our wounds to the Lord and receive the help and healing that only He can give. If I had known this years ago, I never would have spent so many years trying to fight my own battles, or trying to make others pay for the wrongs they did to me. If you are hurting right now and are tempted to vent your anger and frustration against someone, let me encourage you instead to bring these feelings to the Lord in prayer. Ask Him to show you how to rightly handle these emotions, and how to resolve them in a constructive manner. Then receive His wonder-working power to help and heal!

PRAYER

Lord, I thank You that You've given me a spirit of self-control so that I have the power to respond in a Christlike manner when others hurt me. (2 Tim. 1:7 AMP; Gal. 5:23.) Help me to become more like Jesus daily by spending time in Your presence and in Your Word. Thank You that as I handle my anger and frustration in ways that please You, I will come out on top in every situation!

The Benefits of Rebuke

Let a righteous man strike me—it is a kindness; let him rebuke me—it is oil on my head. My head will not refuse it.

PSALM 141:5

I don't know anyone who likes being criticized. I doubt very much that King David really enjoyed it, either. Yet in the above verse, David reveals how he had learned the benefits of being rebuked, especially by a righteous person. He calls being reproved "a kindness" and says that he "will not refuse it." David knew that even if the rebuke was given with the wrong intent, he could still benefit from it. That's true humility, and that's one of the reasons why God called him "a man after my own heart," and why He was able to use this man mightily. Proverbs 29:23 says, "Pride ends in a fall, while humility brings honor." People who are prideful don't take correction very well. Instead of receiving it in a humble manner, they often become angry and offended, rejecting the reproof, even if it was given in genuine love and concern. These people usually end up hurting themselves more than anyone else, and even if they are very gifted believers, God isn't likely to bless or use them the way He would like to. Proverbs 15:31-32 says, "He who listens to a life-giving rebuke will be at home among the wise. He who ignores discipline despises himself, but whoever heeds correction gains understanding." Instead of always seeing correction as something negative, we should try to think of it in terms of being "life-giving," and a way of gaining more wisdom. How we respond to criticism tells a lot about us, especially where our spiritual maturity is concerned.

Psalm 94:12-13 says, "Blessed is the man you discipline, O Lord, the man you teach from your law; you grant him relief from days of trouble." This verse reveals a remarkable biblical principle. One of the primary ways the Lord corrects us is through His Word. If we spend time with God daily, fellowshipping with Him in prayer and Bible study, the Lord will not have to use other people to reprove us as often. But those who neglect spending time in God's Word will suffer frequent correction and criticism from others, simply because they haven't given God much choice in the matter. James 1:29 says, "Man's anger does not bring about the righteous life that God desires." When we respond to criticism with anger, even a reproof that is justified and meant to be constructive will fail to benefit us or our spiritual growth. Some people get angry at correction simply because it enables them to avoid facing their problem and having to do anything about it. The Bible often equates correction with love. Proverbs 27:5 says, "Better is open rebuke than hidden love." And Proverbs 27:6 says, "Wounds from a friend are better than kisses from an enemy!" So we mustn't assume that because someone rebukes us, they don't care about us or they mean us harm. It may be just the opposite. Proverbs 15:12 says, "A mocker resents correction; he will not consult the wise." If we're in a situation where it would be smart for us to ask advice from godly people and we refuse to do so, we may have a problem with pride. We will end

LIVE ON PURPOSE TODAY

Make sure to spend time today—and every day—fellowshipping with the Lord in prayer and Bible study so God will be less likely to need others to reprove you.

up hurting ourselves because we've rejected the help God would have offered us through them. The best way to handle reproof—even if it's not given with good intentions—is to receive it in a Christlike manner and ask God, "Lord, is there any truth to this? Are there some changes I need to make here?" If so, we can count on the Lord to give us the grace we need to become all that He wants us to be.

PRAYER

Lord, whenever I'm criticized or corrected, help me to respond with the right attitude. Surround me with godly people who will hold me accountable. Teach me to spend time with You and Your Word daily so that You won't have to use others to correct me so often. Thank You for doing a mighty work in me so that You can bless and use me in awesome ways!

Loving the Unlovable

If all you do is love the lovable, do you expect
a bonus? Anybody can do that.

MATTHEW 5:46 MESSAGE

When my sons were very young, we used to frequent a little convenience store in our neighborhood that sold some of their favorite snacks. Unfortunately, the lady who worked behind the counter was always cold and unfriendly, and even rude to us. At first I was tempted to avoid the store completely, but something inside of me urged me to "turn the other cheek" and to be kind and gracious to her no matter what. Every time I went into that store and that lady wore a sour face or scowled at me, I would smile and wish her a good day. I was sincere and she knew it. One day when I went in with my two boys, out of the blue she handed them each a delectable treat and refused to let me pay for them. We graciously accepted them and thanked her for her kindness. Shortly after that day we drove into the parking lot and discovered that her store had closed down. It never reopened and we never saw that woman again.

The Lord brought this incident to my remembrance recently to remind me how important it is to be kind to those who are unkind to us. Looking back, I realize that this woman was probably hurting terribly at the time. She knew that she would soon lose her job—even her store—if she was in fact the owner, as I suspect she was. The Lord reminded me that hurting people often hurt others. And it's usually the people who treat us the worst that need the most love, understanding, and kindness from us. I have found that, in most cases, when I treat others with the kindness they withhold from me, I can usually win them over if I don't quit and give up too soon. When that happens, I not only feel good about myself, but I can sense God smiling from ear to ear. Occasionally, though, I encounter people who are steadfastly determined to be miserable, and who try to make everyone around them miserable. In those cases, I eventually have to leave these people to their own devices and to God, refusing to let them steal my peace and joy. Jesus said, "Do you think you deserve credit for merely loving those who love you? Even the godless do that! And if you do good only to those who do you good—is that so wonderful? Even sinners do that much!" (Luke 6:32,33 TLB). The Savior makes it clear that He expects much more from us than He does from the world, and we mustn't think too highly of ourselves when we are good to those who treat us well. He goes on to say, "Love your enemies! Do good to them! Then your reward from heaven will be very great, and you will truly be acting as children of the Most High, for He is kind to the unthankful and to those who are wicked. You must be compassionate, just as your Father is compassionate"

LIVE ON PURPOSE TODAY

Remember, people who treat you the worst are the ones who need your love the most. So be generous today and treat people with the kindness that they may withhold from you. You'll sense God smiling from ear to ear.

(Luke 6:35,36 NLT). Here, Jesus reveals how we can please God and receive great blessings from Him. Remember that we're not given the Holy Spirit to do ordinary things, or to behave like the rest of the world. We're given God's Spirit so that we can do the extraordinary, and that includes responding in a Christlike manner when we're met with unkindness. Do you want to make a real difference for God in this world? This is one way to do it. Do you want God to use you in new and exciting ways? This is a good way to show Him that you're ready. Do you want to walk in a greater level of blessings? Sowing seeds like these will bring you a harvest of rewards you won't receive any other way. I like the way the Message Bible puts it: "I tell you, love your enemies. Help and give without expecting a return. You'll never—I promise—regret it"! (Luke 6:35 MESSAGE).

PRAYER

Lord, I thank You for pouring Your love into my heart by the Holy Spirit so that I don't have to be unkind to those who are unkind to me. (Rom. 5:5.) Help me to remember that people who hurt others are usually hurting themselves. Remind me often that Your Word says, "Pray for those who hurt you" (Luke 6:28 NLT). Thank You for giving me the grace I need to "live a life that Jesus would be proud of"! (Phil. 1:10 MESSAGE).

God's Perfect Timing

For the vision is yet for an appointed time and it hastens to the end [fulfillment]; it will not deceive or disappoint. Though it tarry, wait [earnestly] for it, because it will surely come; it will not be behindhand on its appointed day.

HABAKKUK 2:3 AMP

Almost two years ago my husband, Joe, applied for a job in the company where his friend and former coworker, Rob, was employed. My husband really wanted and needed this position. Even so, we put this job "on the altar," and we asked the Lord to close every door if it wasn't His best for Joe. My husband's interview went so well that Rob told him that the job was his. Nevertheless, doors began closing against Joe, and the job was given to someone else. Even though we were disappointed, we tried to take comfort in the knowledge that the Lord had intervened in order to keep my husband in His perfect will.

Recently, Rob approached Joe with a second opportunity for them to work together. A job which was almost identical to the one that my husband lost had opened up, and though Joe was hesitant to try a second time, Rob convinced him that it was worth a shot. Once again, even though we really wanted this job for Joe, we prayed that God would open and close the right doors so that my husband would be kept in the Lord's perfect will. We were all amazed when every door that seemed closed the first time opened wide. Joe was offered the job, and he accepted.

What made the difference between these two experiences? God's timing. In both instances, my family and I prayed the same way. We asked the Lord to open and close the right doors so that my husband would be in His perfect will at all times. The first time, God closed doors. The second time, He opened them. As we earnestly sought the Lord's wisdom and guidance, He moved mightily to keep us in His will and timing.

There are times when it appears that God is saying "no" to us, but He's actually saying "wait." The Bible often uses phrases like "the appointed time" or "the proper time." Solomon wrote, "There is a proper time and procedure for every matter" (Eccl. 8:6). Ours is not a "hit-or-miss" God. He created us with specific plans and purposes in mind, and His timing is always perfect. Scripture says, "But these things I plan won't happen right away. Slowly, steadily, surely, the time approaches when the vision will be fulfilled. If it seems slow, do not despair, for these things will surely come to pass. Just be patient! They will not be overdue a single day!" (Hab. 2:3 TLB). As long as our trust is in God and we are praying and seeking Him daily, we can be sure that He is busy working behind the scenes to bring our God-given dreams and visions to pass. The Lord instructs us to be patient and not to despair, because He knows that impatience and discouragement can cause us to miss out on His best for us. Sometimes God makes us wait because certain circumstances are not yet right for us. Other times, we're

LIVE ON PURPOSE TODAY

Whether you see the evidence or not, lift your voice today with praise to the Lord for bringing about His best for you. Trust His timing!

the ones who are not yet ready, or someone else involved is not prepared. As long as we are praying and believing God to work all things out for our good (Rom. 8:28), we can trust that He is actively working in our circumstances, in our lives, and in the lives of others. If you are waiting on God for some special blessing or breakthrough today, remember that delays are not necessarily denials. Keep your faith and hope in God, believing that at just the right time He will open doors for you. When He does, you will know without a doubt that it was worth the wait!

PRAYER

Lord, please teach me to always have an attitude that says, "God, if it's not Your will for me, I don't want it!" Help me to realize that even something that is Your will for me, but that is out of Your perfect timing, is still disobedience. Grant me the patience I need to wait upon You for Your absolute best. Thank You that as I keep in step with Your plans for me, my blessings won't be delayed a single day!

From Harm to Healing

{ *You intended to harm me, but God intended it for good to accomplish what is now being done, the saving of many lives.*

GENESIS 50:20 }

The above words belong to Joseph, the son of Jacob. When he was 17 years old, his own brothers sold him to slave traders because he was his father's favorite and they were jealous of him. He was taken to Egypt and eventually imprisoned because of a false accusation. In prison he helped Pharaoh's cup-bearer, who neglected to return the favor, and Joseph spent two more years in jail. When Joseph was 30 years old he interpreted a dream for Pharoah, who made him ruler over all of Egypt. For 13 long years Joseph endured injustice and rejection. Through it all he continued to trust God, who rewarded him with extraordinary blessings. Joseph speaks the above words to his brothers when they meet again after many years. He tells them that though they meant to do him harm, God turned it into good for him and many others. As ruler over Egypt, he was able to prepare the Egyptians for seven years of famine. Even the Israelites, including Joseph's own family, were amply supplied.

Joseph's life is the perfect example of how God can turn the worst kind of adversity into good for His children. Though it was Joseph's brothers who sold him into slavery, it was Satan behind the evil deed. Even after 13 years of mistreatment and misfortune, God's purpose was fulfilled in Joseph's life, and the Lord used him mightily to save others and to glorify Himself. Maybe you've experienced injustice or rejection in your life. Perhaps you've even struggled with feelings of worthlessness. Maybe you feel like God has forgotten you. Joseph must have felt that way, too. But listen to what Jesus says in Luke 18:27: "The things that are impossible with men are possible with God." You can't turn the adversities in your life into something good. Neither can anyone else. But God can. It's one of the things that He does best. If you will place yourself in God's hands and put your trust in Him, He has a special promise for you today. It's in Romans 8:28 and it says, "And we know that in all things, God works for the good of those who love him, who have been called according to his purpose." There isn't anything that's happened to you that God can't turn into your good. Let Him prove it to you. He's only a prayer away.

LIVE ON PURPOSE TODAY

Now that you've prayed this prayer, take a few moments to write down your past hurts and transgressions that come to mind. And then as you look at the paper, forget the past. Tear the paper up, and throw it away. Make today the day that you leave the past behind and move on with God!

PRAYER

Lord, You know all the things I've suffered in my life—the injustice, rejection, and sorrow. Right now, I give them all to You, along with my very life, and I ask that You heal me of all past hurts. Deliver me from a feeling of worthlessness, and give me a new sense of purpose. Take every negative experience in my past and turn it into my good. Thank You for using me to touch others' lives for Your glory!

Be a Blessing and Be Blessed!

> *"As surely as the Lord your God lives," [the widow] replied, "I don't have any bread—only a handful of flour in a jar and a little oil in a jug. I am gathering a few sticks to take home and make a meal for myself and my son, that we may eat it—and die." Elijah said to her, "Don't be afraid. Go home and do as you have said. But first make a small cake of bread for me from what you have and bring it to me, and then make something for yourself and your son. For this is what the Lord, the God of Israel, says: 'The jar of flour will not be used up and the jug of oil will not run dry until the day the Lord gives rain on the land.'"*
>
> 1 KINGS 17:12-14

At God's command, the great prophet Elijah pronounced a drought over all Israel because of the wickedness of King Ahab and his wife, Jezebel. Instead of sending His beloved servant to one of the wealthy citizens of the land for provision, God sends him to a starving widow in Zarephath. When Elijah asks her for some bread and water, she reveals that she only has enough flour and oil to make one last meal for herself and her son. If you had been this widow, what do you think your reaction would have been? I think I might have said something like, "What! Are you crazy? My kid and I are starving to death, and you have the nerve to ask *me* to help *you*?" Oh well. There goes my shot at a miracle. Thankfully, this widow obeyed Elijah and gave him all the provisions she had left in the world. Her act of faith birthed a miracle. God provided for her, her son, and the prophet throughout the entire drought.

I can't tell you why God expected this widow to provide for Elijah. It's just one more example of how God likes to work in ways we don't expect. Perhaps there have been times when God has

LIVE ON PURPOSE TODAY

Out of whatever you have the least of, give today! If you are running low on joy, give some. If you are running short on finances, sow some. Find someone whose life you can touch, and be blessed by being a blessing.

asked you to meet someone's needs, even though you felt you had little or nothing to offer. Maybe there have been times when God asked you to "just be there" for someone who was going through a rough time, and you couldn't help but think, *But God, I have troubles of my own. I can't help them now.* Remember this widow. Remember how God blessed her abundantly because, even in her darkest hour, she reached out in faith to someone in need.

PRAYER

Lord, help me to focus less on my own needs, and to look around me to see the needs of others. Fill my heart with a love like Yours, and take from me the pride and the fear that hinder me from reaching out to them. Use me to touch and change people's lives for their good and Your glory. Thank You for blessing me and making me a blessing!

When Obedience
Brings Trouble

> *Moses returned to the Lord and said, "O Lord, why*
> *have you brought trouble upon this people? Is this why*
> *you sent me? Ever since I went to Pharaoh to speak*
> *in your name, he has brought trouble upon this people,*
> *and you have not rescued your people at all."*
>
> EXODUS 5:22,23

G od had revealed to Moses that He had a plan to rescue the Israelites from Egyptian bondage, and Moses would be His instrument. In obedience to God's instructions, Moses confronted Pharoah and demanded that he let the Lord's people go out into the desert to worship Him. But instead of the expected deliverance resulting from the encounter, Pharoah ordered the Hebrew slaves to produce the same amount of bricks, but this time without the straw they were accustomed to being supplied with. Not only were the Israelites not delivered from their captivity, but their problems grew worse as the result of Moses' obedience to God. Who could blame Moses for crying out to God in frustration?

Have you ever had the experience of obeying God in a situation and then being met with more hardships or problems, instead of the anticipated relief or reward? Did you ever express your confidence in God's promises of provision and deliverance to friends or family, only to have your situation grow worse, so that you feared that others would doubt God's dependability? Take heart, dear one. We've all been there. Perhaps God wants us to focus on obeying Him, rather than on the results of our obedience. In every situation and circumstance, obey God—and then trust Him to take care of the results. The Lord didn't deliver Moses and His people overnight, but He did deliver them. Make no mistake—He'll deliver you, too!

LIVE ON PURPOSE TODAY

Take the time today to renew your mind and encourage your heart by finding two or three Scriptures that promise the rescue you need most. Quote them throughout the day!

PRAYER

Lord, please forgive me for the times I've obeyed You and then grumbled or lost faith because I did not receive the reward or results that I had expected or hoped for. Change my heart and renew my mind so that I will learn to focus on obeying You in everything, without regard for the results. Thank You that Your promises to provide for me and rescue me are true, and that You are faithful!

God's Way Works

Simon answered, "Master, we've worked
hard all night and haven't caught anything.
But because you say so, I will let down the nets."

LUKE 5:5

Peter was a seasoned fisherman. He had fished all night and had caught nothing. Yet this preacher, who obviously knew little about fishing, insisted that he try again. It didn't make sense to Peter and he had his doubts, but when he obeyed Jesus, he witnessed a miracle. The Scripture says "they caught such a large number of fish that their nets began to break."

Did you ever feel like all your efforts in a situation were accomplishing nothing? Maybe you had tried all the ways the "experts" recommended. All the suggestions your friends made. Every course of action that made sense to you. Maybe you've decided that there is no solution to the problem, and you've resigned yourself to living with it. Perhaps the Savior is saying to you today, "You've tried it your way—now try it Mine." God's instructions to us don't always make sense. We're told to give if we want to receive. To forgive, even when it seems unthinkable. To love, even when we're not loved in return. Give your struggles to the Lord, and tell Him you're willing to do things His way this time. Then prepare to see mountains move!

PRAYER

Lord, forgive me for wanting to do things my way. Help me to seek You and Your will in everything that concerns me. Make me willing to obey You, and teach me Your ways, that I may no longer follow my own ways or those of others. Thank You for all the blessings I'll receive as a result!

LIVE ON PURPOSE TODAY

Have you been wrestling and struggling unsuccessfully to handle a situation on your own? If so, it's time to hand it over to God! For your own welfare, ask yourself what practical step you can take to secure your situation into God's hands.

Our Helplessness
Can Lead to Hope

> *When Jesus looked up and saw a great crowd coming toward him,*
> *he said to Philip, "Where should we buy bread for these people to*
> *eat?" He asked this only to test him, for he already had in mind*
> *what he was going to do. Philip answered him, "Eight months'*
> *wages would not buy enough bread for each one to have a bite!"*
>
> JOHN 6:5-7

E ven though Jesus knew ahead of time that he was going to multiply enough loaves and fishes to feed the multitudes, He first tested Philip by asking him what he thought the solution to their food shortage was. Jesus was making a point here. He wanted Philip and the other disciples to acknowledge the fact that there was no human solution to the problem, so that God would get the glory for the miraculous provision that was to come.

Many times it is only after we admit our helplessness that we see God's powerful intervention in our lives. Is there a situation in your life right now that seems hopeless? Commit it to the Lord, and when you do, admit that you need His help and you are depending on Him to come to your aid. Then wait patiently, but with a renewed confidence that He has heard your prayer and is already working out a solution according to His perfect wisdom and plan for you!

PRAYER

Lord, help me not to come to You as a last resort when I am in need. Help me, instead, to seek You first from now on. I need You, Lord, and I'm depending on You to give me the wisdom, strength, and grace I need to be all that You want me to be, and to do all that You want me to do.

LIVE ON PURPOSE

When we get God's Word at work in our situation, we'll have God at work in our situation. Comb through the Bible for three Scriptures that promise your solution and take them prayerfully before the Lord.

New Beginnings

Forget the former things; do not dwell on the past. See, I am doing a new thing! Now it springs up; do you not perceive it.

ISAIAH 43:18,19

Two years ago my older son, Joseph, moved out of our home. Coping with his absence alone would have been difficult enough, but around the same time of his departure, my younger son, John, graduated from high school. John was going to remain at home and attend a local college, and I was grateful for that. But his high school graduation would mark the end of my family's involvement with the Bible club my older son started five years earlier. During those years my life had been filled with countless club-related tasks, including driving teens home from weekly meetings, helping my sons put together Bible lessons, holding parties in my home for the kids, and organizing frequent concert trips. Once it was all over my life began to seem empty, purposeless, and meaningless. Feelings of being unneeded and unwanted overwhelmed me, and I didn't know how to stop the downward spiral I found myself in. During this time I cried out to the Lord in desperation and despair. It was then that He showed me the above verses in Isaiah 43. He revealed to me that He wanted to do a "new thing" in my life, but first I had to "forget the former things" and "not dwell on the past." God's awesome new plans for me would not unfold until I stopped feeling sorry for myself and let go of all the negative emotions associated with my profound sense of loss. I had to determine to put the past behind me and believe that God had wonderful plans ahead for me, or I would never "perceive" the "new thing" He wanted to do in my life. It wasn't easy for me. I kept thinking about all the special times I had shared with my son over the past 20 years, as well as all the wonderful experiences I had had through my involvement with the Bible club. There were times I doubted that I would ever recover from my sense of loss. But as I prayed and depended upon God's grace to heal me and to help me let go of the past, the Lord began to unfold the "new thing" He had planned for me. Today my life is filled with more purpose and meaning than I ever dreamed possible, and I shudder to think of all the blessings I would have missed out on if I hadn't cooperated with God for my deliverance. If you are feeling today that your life is empty, meaningless, or purposeless because of your past experiences or a sense of loss, please know that God has awesome plans for your life. He says, "For I know the plans I have for you—plans to prosper you and not to harm you, plans to give you hope and a future" (Jer. 29:11). It doesn't matter how old you are or what your background is—God is able to fill your life with new purpose and meaning. Start asking Him to do something new and wonderful in your life. Trust Him to begin revealing the "new thing" He has planned for you as you determine to let go of what lies behind and reach out for what lies ahead. Remember that endings pave the way for new beginnings.

LIVE ON PURPOSE TODAY

Take some time today to reflect on your dreams, and write down your top three goals. Keep them in a place where you can refer to them often—in your Bible or nightstand perhaps.
Pray about them, and begin to take steps toward them as the Lord leads you.

Today, be encouraged by this precious promise from God: "Arise [from the depression and prostration in which circumstances have kept you—rise to a new life]! Shine (be radiant with the glory of the Lord), for your light has come, and the glory of the Lord has risen upon you!" (Isa. 60:1 AMP).

PRAYER

Lord, I ask that You give me a new awareness of the awesome plans You have for my life. Help me to stop dwelling on the past, and to let go of all regret, sorrow, and bitterness. Fill my life with new purpose and meaning, and use me to make a difference in people's lives for Your glory. Thank You for a new beginning and a fresh start!

Dealing With Misplaced Fear

The Lord has said to me in the strongest terms: "Do not think like everyone else does. Do not be afraid that some plan conceived behind closed doors will be the end of you. Do not fear anything except the Lord Almighty. He alone is the Holy One. If you fear him, you need fear nothing else. He will keep you safe."

ISAIAH 3:11-14 NLT

This passage was God's warning to the Israelites that if they looked to other nations for protection against their enemies, they would be destroyed. The Lord told His people that if they would fear Him only, and not man, they need fear nothing else because He would be their safety. With all the things in our world today that pose a threat to us, how could God expect us to live free from fear? We begin to understand when we read verse 11: "Do not think like everyone else does." If we think like the world, we will have the same fears, and ultimately, we will seek safety apart from God. Once we do that, we forfeit the divine protection He offers us.

When we feel afraid, we need to ask ourselves what it is that we are afraid of. More than likely, it's a person or persons. Proverbs 29:25 says, "Fear of man will prove to be a snare, but whoever trusts in the Lord is kept safe." The phrase "fear of man" doesn't have to refer to our being afraid of someone harming us. Most often it refers to our fearing man's disapproval. If we allow another person to influence our decisions, apart from God's will, we will not only sacrifice God's best for us, but our safety as well.

LIVE ON PURPOSE TODAY

As an important spiritual exercise, ask yourself today what you are most tempted to fear in life. When you have the answer to that question, you'll know which Scriptures from God's Word are needed to shore up your thinking and renew your mind.

Is there someone whose disapproval you're afraid of? Perhaps it's a family member, friend, teacher, or pastor. Whoever it is, remember that it is only God's disapproval that we should fear, not man's. In everything that concerns you, obey God and let Him take care of the consequences. In Galatians 1:10, the apostle Paul writes, "Am I now trying to win the approval of men, or of God? Or am I trying to please men? If I were still trying to please men, I would not be a servant of Christ." My prayer today is that you will always seek God's approval, rather than man's. When you do, you can be sure that you'll be safe in the arms of a loving and mighty God!

PRAYER

Lord, I ask today that You change my heart and renew my mind so that I will no longer "think like everyone else does." Help me to fear Your disapproval more than that of others from now on. Help me to do it out of a love for You, rather than a fear of the consequences. Thank You for keeping me safe and enabling me to live a fearless life!

When Our Faith Is Tested

Shadrach, Meshach and Abednego replied to the king,
"O Nebuchadnezzar, we do not need to defend ourselves
before you in this matter. If we are thrown into the blazing
furnace, the God we serve is able to save us from it, and
he will rescue us from your hand, O king. But even if he
does not, we want you to know, O king, that we will not serve
your gods or worship the image of gold you have set up."

DANIEL 3:16-18

Shadrach, Meshach, and Abednego were three faithful servants of God who were taken into Babylonian captivity by King Nebuchadnezzar. When the king issued a decree stating that everyone in his kingdom had to bow down and worship his golden idol or be thrown into a fiery furnace, these three young Hebrew men refused. The king was so furious with their disobedience that he ordered that the furnace be turned up seven times hotter than usual. The soldiers who threw the young Hebrews into the furnace were killed instantly. But while Shadrach, Meshach, and Abednego were inside the oven, they were visited by a heavenly deliverer and escaped unharmed. Scholars differ concerning the "fourth man" in the furnace. Some say it was an angel, others a pre-incarnate appearance of Christ. In either case, God rescued His faithful servants from certain destruction.

The above verses have gotten me through some of the most difficult times of my life. They have inspired me to believe in God's miracle-working, delivering power. At the same time, they

LIVE ON PURPOSE

Even in a seemingly hopeless situation, God's Word will always bring you through! Seek out Scriptures that promise deliverance and devote yourself to meditating in them.

have inspired me to commit myself to be faithful to God and trust Him during tests and trials, even if He chooses not to rescue me. Look at it this way—if God rescued us from trouble every time, we wouldn't need faith. Not only that, but many people would end up serving God only because doing so would guarantee them trouble-free lives. The truth is that we will never know for sure on this side of eternity why God sometimes allows His people to suffer adversity. But it's my prayer that you will take comfort in knowing that when you are in the midst of your trials, there will be a "fourth man" with you—and His name is Jesus!

PRAYER

Lord, I must confess that I don't always understand why You often allow those who are devoted to you to experience suffering. Please quiet my doubts and fears with the reassurance that only comes from You. Give me the faith to declare Your ability and willingness to deliver me from harm. But also, give me the grace to stand firm and faithful when You choose not to rescue me. Thank You, Jesus, that when trouble comes, You'll be by my side!

Shut Up and Pray

This is the confidence we have in approaching God:
that if we ask anything according to his will, he hears us.
And if we know that he hears us—whatever we ask—
we know that we have what we asked of him.

1 JOHN 5:14,15

Some years ago my husband, Joe, and his sister had a serious disagreement, and as a result, they stopped speaking to each other. I tried several times to intervene and bring them back together, but every attempt of mine failed. Whenever I tried talking to my husband about reconciling with his sister, I was met with increasing resistance. I finally put the matter in the Lord's hands and told Him that I was counting on His help. I began to earnestly pray for reconciliation, but I didn't talk to my husband about it. One morning Joe confessed to me that he had a dream about making peace with his sister. He began sharing with me how often he thought of her and how he felt like the Lord might be leading him to call her. Finally, the day came when he did just that. His sister wasn't as receptive as he had hoped, but with the Lord's help, Joe lovingly persisted and they have enjoyed a peaceful relationship ever since. For the past ten years my husband has worked part-time for a large tax preparation firm during tax season. He's done this in addition to his full-time job. Every year during tax season our kids and I knew we weren't going to see much of their dad. Besides that, Joe had to work on Sundays, which made it very difficult for us to attend church as a family. I often complained about his second job and pleaded with him to quit. But no matter what I said or did, he refused. This year I decided to put the matter in God's hands, and I began praying earnestly that He would make a way for my husband to leave his part-time job. After several weeks, when Joe began complaining about all the negative changes that were being made in his company, I casually suggested that perhaps it was God's will for him to finally quit. I was stunned when my husband went into work the following day and gave his notice. I had read about the "shut up and pray" principle, and I believed it was the strategy God wanted me to employ in both of these situations. I was relatively certain that I was praying according to God's will, and I claimed God's promise in the verses above. But to be honest, I wasn't completely sure until I witnessed the Lord's supernatural intervention. David prayed, "Set a guard over my mouth, O Lord; keep watch over the door of my lips" (Ps. 141:3). If we pressure people or say the wrong things when we want them to change their behavior or course of action, we can make them more stubborn and resistant. In these cases, we're not helping God; we're hindering Him.

LIVE ON PURPOSE TODAY

Check your heart and see if there is anyone you've been trying to change. If there is, take a moment right now to pray for him or her. Paul's prayer in Ephesians 1:17-23 is a perfect prayer for those who need change in their life.

Often the Lord won't get involved in matters like these until we back off and hand them completely over to Him. If we stop trying to accomplish what only God can, and if we invite Him into the situation through fervent prayer, He will do what we can't. He knows how to reach these people even when we don't, and He can put pressure on them in ways that will turn their hearts toward—not against—Him and us.

If we're ever tempted to harbor bitterness or resentment against the people involved, we must repent and ask for God's forgiveness and help; otherwise our prayers won't be very effective. If you feel like you've tried everything to get someone to change their behavior or course of action and you've gotten nowhere, let me encourage you to entrust the matter to the Lord, "enter His rest," and "cease from your own labors" (Heb. 4:3,10). Persevere in prayer, then be prepared to witness the miracle-working power of God!

PRAYER

Lord, show me when to confront someone about their behavior, and when to just be silent and pray for them. Help me to do my part and to let You do Yours. When I'm tempted to hold anything against anyone, help me to forgive them quickly and thoroughly. Thank You that because of my right-standing with You in Christ Jesus, my prayers shall have "great power and wonderful results"! (James 5:16 TLB).

The Long Arm of the Lord

> But Moses said, "Here I am among six hundred thousand
> men on foot, and You say, 'I will give them meat to eat for
> a whole month!' Would they have enough if flocks and
> herds were slaughtered for them? Would they have
> enough if all the fish in the sea were caught for them?"
> The Lord answered Moses, "Is the Lord's arm too short? You will
> now see whether or not what I say will come true for you."
>
> NUMBERS 11:21-23

When I read this passage, I can't help thinking to myself, *Here's Moses—the man who witnessed countless miracles performed by God, including the cycle of plagues against Pharaoh and his people, and the spectacular parting of the Red Sea—doubting that this same God can provide the Israelites with an ample supply of meat in the wilderness.* And then I feel convicted and think, *But how many times have I seen God do wonderful things in my own life—many times when the odds were stacked against me—and then doubted His ability or willingness to come through for me yet again?*

How many miracles does God have to perform for us before we'll trust Him the way He desires and deserves us to? Fifty? A hundred? I suspect, human nature being what it is, there will always be times when we doubt God, no matter how many miracles He's performed for us in the past. When the Lord said to Moses, "Is the Lord's arm too short?" He was really saying, "Am I powerless to help?" Could He be saying that to you today? Rest assured that the same God who magnificently provided meat for

His people out in the wilderness will provide for your needs, too!

PRAYER

Lord, forgive me for my doubts and fears, especially since You have been so faithful in the past. I pray that, from now on, when I am tempted to doubt, You will increase my faith and grant me a reassurance that will sustain me, even in the most troubling times. Thank You that Your arm is never too short to meet even my greatest needs!

LIVE ON PURPOSE TODAY

Praise the Lord for all the times in the past He came to your rescue. Thank Him for all the wonderful things He has done and for His long arm extended in your behalf. As you rejoice in His goodness of the past, you safeguard your focus on Him for the future.

"Ungodly" Invitations

> *I never sat in the company of revelers, never made merry with them; I sat alone because your hand was on me and you had filled me with indignation.*
>
> JEREMIAH 15:17,18 NLT

In this passage, we learn how the great prophet Jeremiah had endured times of isolation and loneliness because of his devotion to the Lord. Those of us who have shunned invitations to participate in "questionable" social activities because of our commitment to God can really relate to Jeremiah's situation. Some of the things that many people consider harmless "fun" or "entertainment" can carry too high a price tag for the believer. Jesus said, "You are the salt of the earth. But if the salt loses its saltiness, how can it be made salty again? It is no longer good for anything, except to be thrown out and trampled by men" (Matt. 5:13). God has called us to be salt and light to the world. That means that He expects us to stand out, not blend in. The more we blend in with the rest of the world, the less of an impact we will have on it. In Jeremiah 15:19 NLT, God gave His devoted prophet this stern warning: "You are to influence them; do not let them influence you!" If God had to give someone like Jeremiah this admonition, how much more does it apply to us? In 1 Timothy 4:15-16, Paul writes, "Watch your life and your doctrine closely. Persevere in them, because if you do, you will save both yourself and your hearers." How badly do you want to be an effective witness to those around you? Do you have a burning desire to see others receive God's gift of salvation? Then you're going to have to make some serious personal sacrifices, even where your social life is concerned. You're going to have to be more discerning about your social activities, as well as the company you keep.

Our first obligation is to God, not to our friends or family. It's not uncommon for Satan to try to use even our closest loved ones to tempt us to go to places and do things that we know are not God's best for us. And since offering us invitations that don't interest us aren't much of a temptation, the enemy's going to present us with opportunities that seem too good to turn down. "Ungodly" invitations can come in many forms. Movies, concerts, and parties are just a few examples. God wants us to be so sensitive to the leading of His Spirit that we will seek His wisdom and guidance when we make our social plans. Whenever you're confronted with an invitation that you don't have peace about, do not give your consent. Then let the Lord handle the consequences of your refusal. God promised Jeremiah that as a result of his devotion, He would make the prophet His spokesman. (Jer. 15:19.) Jeremiah was faithful, and God kept His promise. If you have a desire to be an instrument of God's power and grace, start saying "no" to some of the invitations that come your way. And know that when you do, you are opening the door for our great God to use you in awesome ways for His glory!

LIVE ON PURPOSE TODAY

Pay special attention to the quality of Christian witness you convey today and every day, and take stock in your activities. If necessary, begin saying, *"No!"*

PRAYER

Lord, whenever I receive invitations of any kind, I ask that You remind me to seek Your approval before I accept. Don't let me forget that my first obligation is to You. Help me to be salt and light to this world so that I can influence others for good, instead of others influencing me in negative ways. Thank You that as I am faithful, You will use me to be a world-changer for Your glory!

Let Go and Let God

While God was testing him, Abraham still trusted in God and His promises, and so he offered up his son....

HEBREWS 11:17 TLB

A few years ago I was at the lowest point in my life as a parent. My older son, Joseph, was at a very rebellious stage, and no matter how I prayed or sought the Lord, nothing seemed to help. As I tuned in to one of my favorite TV ministry programs, I heard the preacher speak Holy Spirit-inspired words about my situation that would change my life and my family forever. I'd like to share those words with you today: "Some of you have kids who are old enough to be hearing from God, and it's time that you offered those children up to the Lord as a sacrifice, and released them into His care. Even if your kids are off track now, let go of them, and let God do something—as you put your trust in Him—to make those children do what's right." I felt so sure that the Lord was speaking these words to me personally that I copied them down and asked Him to give me confirmation. That's when God showed me Hebrews 11:17 TLB: "While God was testing him, Abraham still trusted in God and His promises, and so he offered up his son...." For the past six years I had been praying and standing on God's promises for Joseph. Now it was time for me to offer him up to the Lord as a sacrifice so that He could do in my son's life what He needed to. As fearful as I was, I put Joseph completely in God's hands. Exactly one month later my husband asked our son to leave our home. Even though I felt like my heart was breaking, I knew that this was God's will for us as a family, and I supported my husband's decision. It was time to "let go and let God."

Job 36:15 NLT says, "By means of their suffering, [God] rescues those who suffer. For he gets their attention through adversity." When my son left home, I experienced a period of intense suffering, and during this time God had my undivided attention. As painful as this time was for me, I trusted the Lord to bring good out of it for me and my family. As I sought Him daily through prayer and Bible reading, God showed me that my son had become a kind of idol to me. When He led me to Jesus' words in Matthew 10:37, I felt convicted. "Anyone who loves his son or daughter more than Me is not worthy of Me." Until that moment, I hadn't realized that I had often demonstrated more love and devotion for my son than for God. And God was not about to play second fiddle in the life of one who had professed Christ as their Lord and Savior. I immediately confessed my sin and committed myself to put God first from that moment on, with His help. It was then that God gave me a promise to stand on for the restoration of my family. "The Lord spoke to me again, saying: In Ramah there is bitter weeping—Rachel weeping for her children and cannot be comforted, for they are gone. But the Lord says: Don't cry any longer, for I have heard your prayers and you will see them again; they will come back to you from the distant land of the enemy. There is hope for

LIVE ON PURPOSE TODAY

Check your heart today and make sure that no one holds a larger portion than God Himself. It's best that way— best for you and your family.

your future, says the Lord, and your children will come again to their own land" (Jer. 31:15-17 TLB). This promise from God, along with many others, gave me the encouragement and hope I needed to stand in faith for the healing of my family. Though we've endured some periods of estrangement, tension, and conflict, God has worked wonders in restoring our family. And we continue to seek and trust the Lord to help us please and glorify Him more and more. Last month Joseph married Miriam, a godly young woman who brings out the best in my son and is truly an answer to prayer. I hope and pray this message will encourage you to let go of the loved ones in your life that the Lord is asking you to, so that He may perform the work and wonders that will ultimately bless you and glorify Him.

PRAYER

Lord, reveal to me today how this message applies to my life. Give me the strength and courage I need to let go of the loved ones You want me to. Remind me that as long as I'm holding on to them too tightly, You can't do the good work in them or me that You long to do. Thank You that as I choose to "let go and let God," we will be blessed and You will be glorified!

Needs Vs. Wants

{ *You do not have, because you do not ask God. When you ask,
you do not receive, because you ask with wrong motives....* }

JAMES 4:2,3

One day, after my son made a remark about the pitiful condition of our dining room set, I mentioned to him that I had been praying for a new one. He promptly informed me that new dining room furniture was not a need, and that I shouldn't ask God to replace it for me. At first his comments convicted me and made me feel guilty about my petitions. Then I went to the Lord in prayer and asked Him to give me His view on the situation. Immediately, some of my favorite verses came to mind: "Delight yourself in the Lord and he will give you the desires of your heart" (Ps. 37:4). "He fulfills the desires of those who fear him" (Ps. 145:19). "Ask and you will receive, and your joy will be complete" (John 16:24). God reassured me that He wants to fulfill our needs *and* our desires, and it isn't our job to figure out which is which.

Look at the verses above again in James 4. God says there are some blessings we don't have simply because we didn't ask Him for them. Many times it doesn't even occur to us to ask God for certain things that He is eager to give us—things that He may never allow us to have if we don't seek Him for them. It never even occurred to my son to pray for new furniture. Thank God I didn't have the same attitude he did. These same verses reveal that if we ask for things with the wrong motives, God will not grant them to us. Why did I want a new dining room set? It wasn't because I wanted to show off to my friends and family. It was because my old set was literally falling apart, and it was uncomfortable for my guests, as well as an embarrassment to me. I have new dining room furniture now, and I

LIVE ON PURPOSE TODAY

Take inventory today of your surroundings and decide what is most important for you to trust God for. Then with a heart centered on Him—and full of faith— go to the Lord in prayer.

appreciate it tremendously because I asked God for it and I waited on His timing. These days I have an old car. How many times does it have to break down before I can consider it a "need" and ask God for a newer one? I don't worry about that anymore. I just say, "Lord, I'd like a newer car, but I thank You for the one I have." I feel free to ask God for the desires of my heart, because I love Him with all my heart. I ask for things with the right motives, and I'm willing to wait on God's timing. I can live without nice things. But I can't live without God. With that kind of attitude, I can ask God for the desires of my heart. And so can you.

PRAYER

Lord, teach me how to ask You for all the things You want me to enjoy in this life. Help me to wait on Your perfect timing. Give me a heart that always asks with the right motives. Remind me that even though nice things are desirable, I can live without them. Thank You that You take great pleasure in blessing Your servants! (Ps. 35:27.)

God Cares About the Details

God cares, cares right down to the last detail.

JAMES 5:11 MESSAGE

Recently, it was my friend Peggy's birthday, and I prayed and asked the Lord how I could bless her. I thought of buying her a copy of one of the books I have that I've really enjoyed. But when I got to the store, I felt led to purchase an entirely different book for her instead. I selected a beautiful card with warm sentiments and added some of my own. When I prayed about anything else I could add to her birthday package, it seemed as if the Lord was leading me to put some money in it. My mind immediately thought, *No way. What will she think?* But in the end, I included the money and prayed I was doing the right thing. I found out a few days later that the day my package arrived, Peggy had had a rough day at work. As she drove home that evening, she thought of treating herself to a manicure but quickly gave up the idea when she remembered her many recent expenditures. When she opened my package and discovered the money in her card, she rejoiced and headed straight for the beauty salon with her new book in hand. As it turned out, the book I gave her was filled with just the kind of inspirational stories that delight and encourage her heart.

One of the things I appreciate most about Peggy is that she believes, as I do, that God cares about all the little details of our lives. I know that if I want someone to agree in prayer with me about even the smallest matters concerning me or my family, I can count on Peggy. And I am always amazed at how the Lord continually honors our prayers for even the "small stuff." It saddens me to hear so many believers say things like—"You actually bother God with that kind of stuff?"—whenever they find out that someone is seeking the Lord about something "unimportant." Not only are they missing out on some awesome blessings, but they will never enjoy the depth of intimacy that the Lord longs to share with them. I love the fact that I can consult God when I'm planning on buying a gift for someone. My experience with buying Peggy's gift gave me a new reassurance that this is fact and not fiction. The Lord knows that we are in a constant battle against good and evil in this world, and He's aware of how weary we can get. He longs to encourage us regularly with countless little blessings, as well as with big ones. These little encouragements can give us the lift we need to keep pressing on to the victory when we've been tempted to lose heart. Sometimes I feel like I need a special touch from God, so I pray something like, "Lord, do something new and wonderful in my life!" I may not even know what it is that I want Him to do, but He knows, and He never disappoints me. Don't let anyone tell you that God doesn't care about the little details of your life. There are plenty of believers who are constantly proving otherwise, and I'm one of them. My friend Peggy is another. Jesus said, "Ask, using my name, and you will receive, and your cup of joy will overflow" (John 16:24 TLB). Don't wait a

LIVE ON PURPOSE TODAY

Take a few moments to survey your life and pinpoint anything you previously thought too small to take to the Lord. If you find something, hand it over to Him. God will do the caring!

minute longer. Take the Lord up on His offer today and let Him prove to you once again that He's true to His Word. May this precious promise from God encourage your heart today: "The steps of the godly are directed by the Lord. He delights in every detail of their lives"! (Ps. 37:23 NLT).

PRAYER

Lord, help me to never buy into that lie that says You aren't interested in the little details of my life. Give me a new awareness of just how much You want to be involved in everything that concerns me. Teach me how to pray about the "small stuff," and help me to be sensitive to Your Spirit's leading. Thank You that I will really know You then as I never have before! (Hosea 2:20 TLB.)

Turning the Tables
on the Enemy

{ *As far as I am concerned, God turned into
good what you meant for evil.* }

GENESIS 50:20 NLT

Several years ago my husband and I took our sons to a local
amusement park. My boys were big baseball fans at the time
and they wanted to use the automatic pitching machines so
they could practice their swing. Unfortunately, my son John was hit
squarely on his arm with one of the pitches. Immediately, his arm
began to swell and discolor ominously. After reporting the injury to
the park, we headed for the hospital. On the way there I began
claiming Psalm 34:20, which says, "He protects all his bones, not
one of them will be broken." When we arrived at the hospital
emergency room, we met a mother and her son, who had fallen off
his bicycle and injured his arm. Chills ran down my spine when I
found out that this boy had not only injured the same arm as my
son, but in exactly the same place. The only difference seemed to
be that this boy's arm wasn't nearly as swollen or discolored as
John's. A short time later my family and I were shocked when the
boy came out of the examination room with a cast on his arm,
which was indeed broken. Immediately, fear swept over me, and I
confess that my faith wavered for a few moments. My initial
thought was, *This boy's arm doesn't look half as bad as John's, and his is
badly broken, so how can my son's not be broken?!* As I claimed Isaiah
11:3—"He will not judge by what he sees with his eyes or decide

by what he hears with his ears"—I felt the peace of God quiet my heart and mind. Moments later doctors examined x-rays of my son's arm and could find no trace of a break—not even the slightest fracture. My family and I still marvel over the miracle of that day, as well as God's faithfulness to His Word.

God used this experience to teach me about some of the strategies Satan employs against believers. When my family and I arrived at the hospital emergency room that day, the devil was counting on me to let go of my faith in God and His Word when I saw the other boy with a cast on his arm. As it turned out, I was tempted to doubt and disbelieve, especially because the feelings of fear I experienced were so sudden and severe. But once I shook off those feelings and took my stand in faith, God honored my decision and increased my strength to stand firm. I can't prove that the outcome of this situation would have been different if I had given in to my fears and doubts, but I believe with all my heart that my "faith decision" made all the difference. It's not unusual for Satan to put people and situations in our path to try to

LIVE ON PURPOSE TODAY

Perhaps the devil has tried to confuse or trick you with symptoms or circumstances. Put him in his place. Decide right this minute that you will walk by faith, and God will back you all the way to victory!

get us to doubt God and His Word. And it's nothing new, either. He's been operating this way since the Garden of Eden. But believers don't have to be ignorant of his tactics. The Bible says that we can gain an awareness of the enemy's schemes that can keep us from getting caught in his snares. (2 Cor. 2:11.) As we seek God daily through prayer, praise, and the reading of His Word, He will equip us with everything we need to defeat Satan and his gang. Then, when the devil tries to set us up for a fall, we can witness our Mighty Warrior King turning the tables on our foes and turning our "curses" into blessings. (Deut. 23:5.) That day at the hospital, Satan tried to use that other boy's injury to discourage and defeat me. Instead, God used it to highlight His miracle-working power. The next time you're faced with a similar situation, take your stand in faith, knowing and declaring—"This is all going to turn out for my good!" (Phil. 1:19 TLB).

PRAYER

Lord, help me to become more aware of Satan's tactics so that I won't be an easy target for his attacks. Teach me how to walk by faith and not by sight. (2 Cor. 5:7.) Show me how to cooperate with You to turn the tables on the devil when he comes against me. Thank You for turning every attack of the enemy into my good!

"Amazing" Faith

> *And without faith it is impossible to please God, because*
> *anyone who comes to him must believe that he exists*
> *and that he rewards those who earnestly seek him.*
>
> HEBREWS 11:6

The above verse reveals how our faith pleases God and moves Him to respond to us. Read through the Gospels and you'll see that almost every time Jesus healed or rescued someone, He told them, "Your faith has healed you." Or, "Your faith has saved you." He pointed to their faith so that they would know that it was their belief in God that played a part in receiving their miracle. There are only two places in the Bible where we're told that Jesus was "amazed." One is in Luke 7:9, where Jesus heals a centurion's ailing servant. The Roman believed that the Master didn't even need to be present to heal the boy, and this so "amazed" Jesus that He said, "I tell you, I have not found such great faith even in Israel." And in Mark 6:5-6, where the Savior is rejected by the people in His hometown, the Scripture says, "He could not do any miracles there, except lay his hands on a few sick people and heal them. And he was amazed at their lack of faith."

The Bible has a lot to say about faith. Ephesians 2:8 says that we are "saved by grace through faith." So we know that our very salvation depends on faith. Scripture also tells us, "We live by faith, not by sight" (2 Cor. 5:7). And, "The righteous will live by faith" (Rom. 1:17). So we know that we are to live our daily lives by faith in God. And though we're told in Ephesians 2:9 that our faith is a gift from God, the Bible also says that "faith comes by hearing, and hearing by the word of God" (Rom. 10:17). Therefore, our faith can be increased each time we study the Scriptures, listen to good preaching and teaching, or memorize a new verse. The more time we spend in God's Word and the more we get to know Him personally, the more our faith will abound. But just hearing the Word isn't enough.

LIVE ON PURPOSE TODAY

Since Romans 10:17 says, "faith comes by hearing, and hearing by the word of God," be quick to hear God's Word today! Dwell on Scriptures that answer your need, and faith will supernaturally arise in your heart and enable you to receive God's best!

Hebrews 4:2 warns us that God's Word will have "no value" to us if we don't "combine it with faith." And if our faith is genuine, it will produce righteous deeds. James states that "faith by itself, if it is not accompanied by action, is dead" (James 2:17). Paul says it this way: "The only thing that counts is faith expressing itself through love" (Gal. 5:6). And how does the Bible define faith? It says, "[Faith] is the confident assurance that something we want is going to happen. It is the certainty that what we hope for is waiting for us, even though we cannot see it up ahead" (Heb. 11:1 TLB). My prayer for you today is that you may always have this kind of faith, and that you may receive all that God has in store for you!

PRAYER

Lord, grant me the kind of great faith that pleases and "amazes" You. Give me a growing passion for Your Word and Your presence. Cause my faith to be genuine so that it may be expressed through love and produce good deeds. Thank You for helping me to receive all that You have for me!

Four Steps to Success

Several years ago I heard a godly man offer some advice about how we can enjoy more of the peace and joy that the Lord wants us to have, even in the midst of trouble and uncertainty. He said that if we will make the following statements our personal declarations, and if we will practice the principles behind them, we will gain the victory in every trial we encounter. If we look at each statement in the light of Scripture, we can see that they are all based on sound biblical principles.

1. **"I'm not going to worry about that."** If you've spent any time reading or listening to Scripture, you've undoubtedly become acquainted with the apostle Paul's famous words in Philippians 4: "Don't worry about anything; instead, pray about everything. Tell God what you need, and thank Him for all He has done. If you do this, you will experience God's peace, which is far more wonderful than the human mind can understand. His peace will guard your hearts and minds as you live in Christ Jesus" (Phil. 4:6,7 NLT). Anxiety and worry are rooted in fear, and fear will hinder our faith and trust in God. It will also cause us to lose our sense of direction and make it harder to hear God's "still, small voice." If you're worrying about something, perhaps you need to pray about it more. Keeping it before God in prayer will help you focus more on Him and His abilities, and less on yourself and your inabilities.

2. **"I'm not going to try to figure that out."** One of the hardest things I've had to learn as a true believer in Christ is that I must no longer try to solve my problems my own way.

Instead, I must turn to my divine Problem Solver and depend on Him to show me the way. He tells us, "My thoughts are not your thoughts, neither are your ways My ways. As the heavens are higher than the earth, so are My ways higher than your ways and My thoughts than your thoughts" (Isa. 55:8,9). Our thinking is severely limited, while God's is not. Even when we can't find a single solution to our problem, God has more than a million ways to solve it. But He may not reveal the answer until we stop wrestling with the matter and leave it in His hands.

3. **"I'm not going to try to make something happen."** When we're in a trial and it seems like God isn't moving fast enough to suit us, it can be tempting to try to "kick down doors." But we'd be wise to remember that getting ahead of God and trying to make our own way can not only delay our blessings, but keep us from receiving God's best. The fact is that we are more likely to make mistakes when we fail to wait on God, than when we fail to move on His cue. I like to say, "If in doubt, wait." Isaiah had the right idea when he wrote, "The Lord is a faithful God. Blessed are those who wait for Him to help them" (Isa. 30:18 NLT).

4. **"I'm going to trust God!"** Heeding this single foundational biblical principle will help us to avoid all of the obstacles that the previous three statements are designed to overcome. If we're trusting God, we're much less likely to worry, to try to figure things out for ourselves, or to try to make something happen on our own. Scripture says, "Trust in the Lord with all your heart; do not depend on your own understanding. Seek His will in all you do, and He will direct your paths" (Prov. 3:5,6 NLT). If we will turn to God and seek His perfect will for

LIVE ON PURPOSE TODAY

Today, write down these four principles and keep them where you can refer to them often. Make them your personal declarations, and purpose to practice the principles behind them.

us in every situation—laying aside our own pre-conceived notions and solutions—we can depend on Him to lead us in the paths of His very best blessings. Best of all, we can have peace and joy while we wait for the Lord's answer, resting in the knowledge that our concerns are in the hands of a mighty and loving God!

PRAYER

Lord, in times of turmoil and uncertainty, help me to put my wholehearted trust in You and Your goodness. Guard me from worry and anxiety, and from trying to figure things out on my own. Teach me how to wait on You and Your perfect timing in everything. Thank You that as I trust and seek You every step of the way, my success is guaranteed!

Prepare for Promotion

{ *Do not despise this small beginning, for the eyes of the Lord rejoice to see the work begin....* }

ZECHARIAH 4:10 TLB

A small remnant of Jewish exiles had returned to their homeland after decades of Babylonian captivity. God instructs them to rebuild their temple and their nation. But they become discouraged because of hostilities from their enemies and the realization that the rebuilt temple will not be as great as the previous one, built by King Solomon. The Lord speaks the above words to His weary servants to give them hope and encouragement so that they will continue their God-given task. He tells them that even though it seems like a small beginning, He rejoices in seeing them set to work.

Sometimes God assigns us small tasks which can seem insignificant to us. But in God's sight, there are no unimportant tasks in His kingdom. Sometimes the Lord expects us to prove our faithfulness in little matters before He gives us larger assignments. In Matthew 25:24, Jesus says, "You have been faithful with a few things; I will put you in charge of many things." The Lord is teaching us here that if we will be faithful in the duties He assigns us, promotion will be our reward. At times we can become tempted to promote ourselves, but God's Word makes it clear that job belongs to the Lord. "For promotion and power come from nowhere on earth, but only from God. He promotes one and deposes another" (Ps. 75:6,7 TLB). Perhaps God has given you

LIVE ON PURPOSE TODAY

Is there a task—large or small—that you know in your heart the Lord has asked of you? Set about its completion without delay and set yourself up for promotion from Him!

work to do and you feel as though it has little value or that it's having little impact. Maybe you're receiving very little thanks or recognition. Or you're being met with more resistance than cooperation. Perhaps a previous task the Lord had given you was more appealing than the one you're involved with now. But God doesn't take pleasure in our work for Him only if it's big and important. He rejoices when we do the job He's given us, no matter what the size or significance. If you'll faithfully do the work the Lord's called you to do right now, He will promote you when it will benefit you most. Take heart, for today God's promise to you is—"Humble yourselves, therefore, under God's mighty hand, that he may lift you up in due time"! (1 Peter 5:6).

PRAYER

Lord, forgive me when I feel dissatisfied with the work You've given me to do. Cause me to realize that there are no insignificant tasks in Your kingdom. When I'm tempted to try to promote myself instead of waiting on You, remind me that my efforts will be fruitless in the end. Help me to recognize the jobs You've committed to me and to carry them out faithfully. Thank You that at the proper time, You will reward me with promotion!

God-Pleasers Vs. Man-Pleasers

Am I now trying to win the approval of men, or of God?
Or am I trying to please men? If I were still trying
to please men, I would not be a servant of Christ.

GALATIANS 1:10

The above verse, written by the apostle Paul, warns us that if we are to be true servants of God, we must seek the Lord's approval, rather than man's. Very often God's will and man's are opposed to each other, and here's where the tension arises. Jesus said, "What is highly valued among men is detestable in God's sight" (Luke 16:15). God and man have very different value systems, and we are expected to make right choices, even in tough situations. In Luke 12:48, Jesus tells us, "From everyone who has been given much, much will be demanded; and from the one who has been entrusted with much, much more will be asked." As children of God, we are equipped with the power of the Holy Spirit to live by God's standards, not the world's. The Bible assures us that our God is a just God, and He will never give us unattainable goals to strive for. When we supply the will, He supplies the power. Exodus 23:2 says, "Do not follow the crowd in doing wrong." Jesus said, "Unless you are faithful in small matters, you won't be faithful in large ones" (Luke 16:10 NLT). Don't be deceived into thinking that God doesn't care about the little details of our daily lives. He cares very much, and He expects us to be faithful. Proverbs 25:26 says, "If the godly compromise with the wicked, it is like polluting a fountain or muddying a

LIVE ON PURPOSE TODAY

No one can answer these questions better than you: Do you claim to know God but deny Him with your actions? Do you work to please men more than God? If you answered yes, purpose that today is a day of change!

spring." Not only can our compromise harm our fellowship with God, but it can damage our witness and cost us an opportunity to lead others to the Lord. It's been said that, "People may doubt what you say, but they will believe what you do." Instead of just telling them about Jesus, we need to show them Jesus! We're always appalled when we hear the biblical account of Peter denying Jesus. But look what the apostle Paul says in Titus 1:16: "They claim to know God, but by their actions they deny him." We're no better than Peter when we choose to live our own way, rather than God's. The Bible says that "friendship with the world is hatred toward God" (James 4:4). God's not going to settle for a superficial commitment from us. We have a higher calling on our lives, and it's the Lord's desire to use us for His glory. But He can't use us if we won't submit to His ways and plans for us. In 1 Timothy 1:12, Paul says, "I thank Christ Jesus our Lord, who has given me strength, that he considered me faithful, appointing me to his service." God has promised to reward our faithfulness by giving us opportunities to serve Him. But there are other rewards for choosing to please God rather than people. When we make it our life's goal to please the Lord, the result is joy, peace, and fulfillment. On the other hand, whenever we try to please other people, we experience frustration, disappointment, and emptiness. The truth is that living to please God is the only decent way to live. My prayer for you today is that you will have the same spirit that Peter and the other disciples did when they declared, "We must obey God rather than men"! (Acts 5:29).

PRAYER

Lord, forgive me for the times I chose to please other people instead of You. Give me the strength and courage I need to resist the temptation to win the approval of others. Help me to be faithful in little things so that You can trust me to be faithful in bigger ones. Thank You for rewarding my faithfulness with wonderful opportunities to serve You!

Don't Look Back—or Ahead

Therefore, do not worry about tomorrow, for tomorrow will worry about itself. Each day has enough trouble of its own.

MATTHEW 6:34

Jesus makes it clear here that He doesn't want us worrying about the future. A certain amount of planning is okay, as long as it's done with God's wisdom and guidance. But worrying is another story. It's not only nonproductive, but it can be destructive, too. When Jesus prayed the Lord's Prayer for His disciples, He said, "Give us this day our daily bread." Notice He didn't ask for enough bread for a year, a month, or even a week. When the children of Israel were in the desert those forty years, God provided manna for them daily. But He gave them strict orders to gather only what they needed for that day. If they attempted to gather more, it would decay. God wants to be our Provider, and He wants us to depend on His care and provision daily.

These principles don't just apply to our material needs, but to our spiritual needs as well. If you belong to the Lord and you depend on His grace to live each day, you have only the grace you need for today, whatever it may bring. You don't have the grace to live in the past. And you don't have the grace to live in the future. That's why when you live in the past, you will suffer regret and torment. And if you live in the future, you will be plagued with anxiety and fear. Eventually, your mind and body will pay the price. But if you live each day depending on God and His provision and grace, you will experience an inner peace and joy, no matter what the circumstances. Instead of looking ahead or behind, look up into the blessed face of the Savior—and He will make your cup overflow!

PRAYER

Lord, help me not to live in the past or worry about tomorrow. Give me the grace I need each day to face all my responsibilities and challenges with confidence and courage. Teach me how to depend on You and trust in You so that I'll never have to be fearful of what the future may bring. Thank You that You're all I'll ever need!

LIVE ON PURPOSE TODAY

Determine to keep yourself in "today"! If you catch yourself harboring regrets, you've slipped into yesterday. If you catch yourself in anxiety, you've leaped into tomorrow. Anchor yourself to God's Word where there's plenty of grace for today.

Grace for the Guilty

"Now the king of Aram had ordered his chariot commanders, "Do not fight with anyone, small or great, except the king of Israel." When the chariot commanders saw Jehoshaphat, they thought, "This is the king of Israel." So they turned to attack him, but Jehoshaphat cried out, and the Lord helped him.

2 CHRONICLES 18:30,31

King Jehoshaphat was king of Judah, and he had a heart for God. But he unwisely made an alliance with evil King Ahab of Israel. When their armies attacked the Arameans, Ahab shrewdly disguised himself, while insisting that Jehoshaphat wear his royal robes. Consequently, the Arameans—who were ordered to kill only the king of Israel—mistook Jehoshaphat for Ahab, and they tried to kill him. Jehoshaphat cried out to the Lord, who saved His servant from destruction.

This message is good news today for those of us who have a heart for God but sometimes miss the mark. Are you in financial trouble today because of poor planning or foolish spending? Did you get involved in a relationship that was out of God's will for you? Are you overweight today because of poor eating habits? Maybe you've adopted the attitude, "I've made my bed, now I'll have to lie in it." You may feel like you deserve to suffer the consequences of your mistake, and you don't even feel like you can ask God for help. Jehoshaphat made a terrible mistake, but when faced with the consequences of his actions, he cried out to God and was rescued. No matter how great your sin, turn to the Lord today and receive His mercy and grace. In John chapter 9 of The Message Bible, Jesus speaks some words which I pray will be a comfort to you: "You're looking for someone to blame.... Look instead for what God can do"!

LIVE ON PURPOSE TODAY

Do you feel that you've missed the mark in some way? It's so important to look instead at what God can do! Search God's Word today for Scriptures that will infuse you with strength to forge a better path.

PRAYER

Lord, sometimes I feel so guilty when I know I've done wrong that it's difficult for me to seek You afterwards. The next time I fail You, help me to turn to You right away for forgiveness and help. Please don't let my guilt or pride come between us. Give me a pure heart and a steadfast spirit. Thank You for Your promise to continue the work You've begun in me!

Pursuing Peace in
Our Families

Without wood a fire goes out;
without gossip a quarrel dies down.

PROVERBS 26:20 NIV

This Scripture not only changed my life, it changed my entire family. I was raised in an environment where criticism and sarcasm were prevalent, even though my parents loved me and my sisters very much. By the time I discovered this Scripture several years ago, decades of grudges, gripes, and ill feelings had accumulated. My siblings and I had children of our own, and three generations in my family had learned to live with strife and dissension. Once I became a committed Christian, I became increasingly uncomfortable with the gossip and sarcasm. God showed me the above verse and made it clear to me that I would have to take the initiative to bring about change in my family. The Living Bible version of this verse says, "Fire goes out for lack of fuel, and tensions disappear when gossip stops." Every time one of my relatives criticized or slandered someone else in my family and I joined in, I was adding fuel to the fire that was destroying the peace and harmony of my household. God instructed me to stop adding to the strife in my family by refusing to participate in any malicious talk against my relatives. When I was personally attacked or criticized, the Lord helped me to quickly forgive the offender and to resist responding with a hurtful retort. It wasn't easy and the change didn't happen overnight, but my obedience brought about a healing in my entire family that established a peace, unity, and harmony that is an awesome testimony to the power and truth of God's Word.

If you're tired of the strife in your family and you want it to change, I can tell you from experience that you can make a difference. But you've got to be committed, and you've got to rely on God's grace, because the devil isn't going to make it easy for you. Satan is determined to create strife and division in our families because he knows that the fullness of God's blessings are bestowed upon those who dwell in unity and harmony. (Ps. 133:1,3.) He also knows that "a home filled with argument and strife is doomed" (Luke 11:17 TLB). But if you are a child of God, you are equipped with Holy Spirit power to overcome the enemy's schemes. The Bible tells us, "Work hard at living in peace with others" (Ps 34:14; 1 Peter 3:11 NLT). If you're serious about wanting peace in your family, you're going to have to work hard at it. You're going to have to "make allowance for each other's faults and forgive the person who offends you." If you can't do it for any other reason, then do it simply because "the Lord forgave you" (Col. 3:13 NLT). When it's absolutely necessary to confront a family member about their behavior, don't talk about them behind their back, but "speak the truth in love" (Eph 4:15). Make an effort to speak only words that encourage, build up, and benefit others. (Eph. 4:29.) And pray for your family. Your prayers can move the mighty hand of God in awesome ways. Rest assured that the Lord will honor you for your faithfulness, obedience, and love. My prayer for you is that today you'll take the first step toward bringing healing to your household and discover for yourself the heavenly rewards of a family dwelling in peace!

PRAYER

LIVE ON PURPOSE TODAY

As unspectacular as it sounds, sometimes the most spiritual thing you can do is just to be quiet! Look for an opportunity today when the Holy Spirit would lead you to do just that.

Lord, give me a holy determination to initiate healing in my household, and show me how to take the first step. When I'm tempted to participate in behavior that produces strife, remind me that I have the Holy Spirit power to make a difference. Make me quick to forgive and help me to always speak the truth in love. Thank You for blessing my family with peace and harmony as a result!

The Power of God's Word

The Word of God is full of living power.
It is sharper than the sharpest knife, cutting deep
into our innermost thoughts and desires.

HEBREWS 4:12 NLT

I once read a true story about how a minister spoke God's Word over a friend in the hospital and witnessed its powerful effect on the patient's heart monitor, as well as on the patient herself. Here was modern technology recording and confirming the inherent power in God's Holy Word.

I'm convinced that if believers had a real awareness of just how powerful God's Word is, they would pay more attention to it. When Joshua was taking over Moses' job, God told him to meditate on His Word day and night. The Lord told Joshua that this was how he would be able to perform the will of God and be prosperous and successful. (Josh. 1:8.) And in Proverbs 4:20-22, the Lord says that His Word is life and health to those who pay attention to it. If you're willing to invest some time and energy reading, memorizing, and meditating on the Word of God, you can experience dramatic, positive changes in every area of your life. Let me share with you some simple but powerful principles that the Lord has shown me in recent years.

We can honor God by quoting and meditating on His Word three ways: (1) by putting a verse in prayer form, (2) by making it a declaration of faith, and (3) by turning it into an expression of praise. For example, each day I pray, "Lord, order my steps this day," which is based on Psalm 37:23 KJV. Then throughout the day I reaffirm God's answer to my prayer for guidance by declaring, "My steps are ordered by the Lord!" If doubt and fear begin to assail me, I encourage myself by praising Him for the answer with, "Thank You, Lord, that my steps are ordered by You!" If I have a need, I claim Philippians 4:19 and quote it according to my specific need. "Thank You, Lord, that You supply all my job needs!" I have used this verse to seek God for every conceivable need, including financial, healing, material, and social needs. I combine my faith with my declarations, according to Hebrews 4:2, and as a result, rest and peace flood my mind and heart. God's Word has the ability to build our faith, renew our minds, and change our hearts. If we don't meditate on God's truths

LIVE ON PURPOSE TODAY

Declare God's Word as truth over error in your life today and honor God by quoting and meditating on His Word in the three ways shared: Put a verse in prayer form, make it a declaration of faith, and turn it into an expression of praise.

day and night, we will be easy targets for Satan's deceptions. Declaring God's Word is not mind over matter—it's truth over error. Jesus used Scripture to defeat Satan when he came to tempt the Savior in the wilderness, and we can do the same thing. (Luke 4:1-12.) Each day of our lives we have two choices—we can meditate on God's promises, or we can meditate on our problems. Meditating on God's Word can bring peace, joy, life, and health. Meditating on our problems can cause anxiety, fear, despair, and sickness. The Bible tells us to "be imitators of God" (Eph. 5:1). Do you think God is wringing His hands, wondering what He's going to do about our problems? No way. The Bible says He's "watching over His Word to perform and fulfill it" on our behalf (Jer. 1:12). So let's give Him something to work with. Let's honor our God by letting Him hear His precious Word on our lips day and night, for only then will we be prosperous and successful for His glory!

PRAYER

Lord, fill my heart with a growing passion for Your Word. Help me to believe, declare, and act upon it for my good and Your glory. Show me how to apply Your truth to every area of my life. Thank You, Lord, that Your Word is true and You are true to Your Word!
(John 17:17; Heb. 11:11 AMP.)

Saying "No" to Self-Pity

{ *The bread of idleness (gossip, discontent, and self-pity)*
she (the virtuous woman) will not eat. }

PROVERBS 31:27 AMP

I recently went through some difficulties that got me so discouraged that I found myself wrestling with feelings of self-pity. Years ago I might have played some sad songs and cried my eyes out, deriving a sort of perverse satisfaction from my misery. But this time I prayed and asked the Lord to help me resist these negative emotions. That's when He reminded me about some teaching I heard years ago about self-pity. I once heard a godly man say, "God is concerned about your hurt, but He doesn't want *you* concerned about it." This man went on to say that the reason self-pity is so destructive is that pride is at the root of it, and it causes us to focus too much on ourselves. I looked *self-pity* up in the dictionary and found the following definition: "Pity for oneself, especially pity that is self-indulgent or exaggerated."[3]

Psychiatrists have an interesting name for people who habitually indulge in self-pity—it's "injustice collector." These are the folks who are constantly dwelling on their hurts and hardships— whether real or imagined—and they enjoy thinking about them and talking about them. They lovingly collect and number each and every offense that others commit against them, and they search out people who will sympathize with them and commiserate with them. All this keeps the focus on themselves, which is what they want most. But this isn't God's way. He instructs us to walk in the God-kind of love, which is "not self-seeking," and which "keeps no record of wrongs" (1 Cor. 13:5). This is not to say that we should ignore or deny when we're being mistreated, but that we should take constructive action to see that we're treated with proper respect, or to remove ourselves from harm's way, rather than sit idly by, feeling sorry for ourselves. Self-pity isn't just nonproductive—it's destructive. It can lead to bitterness, unforgiveness, and resentment. It doesn't bring people together— it divides them. And these are some of the reasons why Satan works so hard to get us to focus on our wounds, rather than the cure—which is the love and wisdom of God. Throughout the pages of the Bible, God tells us again and again that He wants us to bring our hurts and sorrows to Him so that *He* can comfort us. He not only wants to be our Comforter, but our Vindicator. (Ps. 135:14.) If we'll let Him, He will defend us and fight our battles for us, leading us to victory every time. He tells us in His Word, "I, the Lord, love justice. I hate robbery and wrong-doing. I will faithfully reward my people for their suffering…" (Isa. 61:8 NLT).

LIVE ON PURPOSE TODAY

Survey your heart and make sure that you're walking in forgiveness. That done, offer thanksgiving to the Father and enumerate the many blessings He has bestowed on you.

A good antidote for self-pity is forgiveness. As we forgive those who offend us, we can let go of our negative emotions and ill-feelings toward others, and we can receive the comfort and healing that can only come from God. Scripture says, "In all their suffering He also suffered, and He personally rescued them. In His love and mercy, He redeemed them. He lifted them up and carried them through all the years" (Isa. 63:9 NLT). God hurts when we hurt, and He wants to be our Deliverer. But we can block His efforts to comfort and rescue us when we insist on holding on to our feelings of resentment, bitterness, and unforgiveness. As we choose to forgive, we open the door to God's involvement, and all the blessings and provisions that entails. Another good antidote for self-pity is thankfulness. The Bible says, "Thank [God] in everything [no matter what the circumstances may be, be thankful and give thanks], for this is the will of God for you [who are] in Christ Jesus" (1 Thess. 5:18 AMP). No matter what is going on in our lives, we always have reason to give thanks to God and praise Him. Nothing is more offensive to God than our dwelling on our misfortunes and losses, and neglecting to recognize and enumerate all of the blessings He bestows on us daily.

Helen Keller said, "Self-pity is our worst enemy and if we yield to it, we can never do anything good in the world." We have been chosen by God, not just to live eternally with Him in heaven, but to make a difference for Him while we're still here on earth. Let's not allow self-pity to neutralize all the good we can do in this world in the name of Jesus.

PRAYER

Lord, please alert me whenever I begin to feel sorry for myself. Keep me from being overly-sensitive and self-absorbed, and teach me to bring all of my hurts and hardships straight to You. When I do, heal and comfort me the way that only You can. Give me the grace I need to forgive others quickly and thoroughly, and to praise You in all things. Thank You that as I resist self-pity in the power of Your Spirit, I will be rewarded by a gracious and grateful God!

Let Your Light Shine

You are the light of the world. A city on a hill cannot be hidden. Neither do people light a lamp and put it under a bowl. Instead they put it on its stand, and it gives light to everyone in the house. In the same way, let your light shine before men, that they may see your good deeds and praise your Father in heaven.

MATTHEW 5:14-16

At a family gathering a few years ago, I couldn't help overhearing a discussion between my son John and a friend of the family. They were talking about a movie that was currently in the theaters and had a soundtrack of popular songs. When my son voiced his disapproval of the album because one of the song titles was an obscenity, I heard this friend exclaim, "Lighten up, John!" What was this friend saying to my son? She was basically saying, "C'mon, John, stop being so serious—and start thinking the way the rest of us do!"

Why do some folks—Christians and non-Christians alike—get so indignant when someone like John takes a stand against the popular culture? It makes them feel uncomfortable. It's like shining a spotlight on their questionable behavior for all the world to see. Jesus said that He wanted His followers to be salt and light to the world around them. (Matt. 5:13-16.) Why? Because it's the only way we can make a real difference for God on this earth. The apostle Paul wrote, "Have nothing to do with the fruitless deeds of darkness, but rather expose them" (Eph. 5:11). Naturally, we can use words to expose the sin around us, but there's an even better way. We can expose the works of darkness by our actions. There's an old saying that goes like this: "People may not believe what you say, but they'll believe what you do!" When mere words don't have an impact on the people around us, our Christlike behavior often can. In the same passage of Scripture, Paul goes on to say, "But when the light shines on them, it becomes clear how evil these things are. And where your light shines, it will expose their evil deeds" (Eph. 5:13,14 NLT). Every time that you and I "go along with the flow" of popular culture, our light for Christ dims and we lose an opportunity to draw others to Him. That's one reason why Paul continues with, "Be very careful then, how you live—not as unwise but as wise, making the most of every opportunity, because the days are evil" (Eph. 5:15,16).

LIVE ON PURPOSE TODAY

All day long, be on the lookout for an opportunity to be a bold witness for Jesus Christ—a bold witness with a shining light. Allow your words and actions to uphold Bible standards even in a dark world.

The following verse gets to the heart of the matter: "Therefore, do not be foolish, but understand what the Lord's will is" (Eph. 5:17). The only way we're going to be able to live a life that's pleasing to God, and one that will impact others for His kingdom, is to have a working knowledge of His Word. How did John know that the profane song title on that movie soundtrack was offensive to God? Because he was familiar with the Scripture that says, "But among you there must not be even a hint of sexual immorality, or of any kind of impurity, or of greed, because these are improper for God's holy people. Nor should there be obscenity, foolish talk or coarse joking, which are out of place, but rather thanksgiving" (Eph. 5:3,4). John didn't just have head knowledge of these verses, but he was applying them to his life and walking them out, instead of just talking about them. And people take notice. When John's at work and everyone around him is cursing and blaspheming, he refuses to join in. He doesn't hit people over the head with his Bible, but he lets his light shine through his words and actions. And he stands out in a crowd. Yes, there's a price to be paid when we live our lives for God. And there are untold sacrifices that we have to make daily. But the rewards far outweigh them all. Just ask John. Because of his faithfulness, the Lord is using him to touch the lives of millions of people each year for His glory. And if you were to ask my son, he'd tell you that he wouldn't want to live any other way. The next time you take a bold stand for the Lord and someone says to you, "Lighten up!"—don't forget that that's your cue to let your light shine!

PRAYER

Lord, give me the strength, the wisdom, and the courage I need to "go against the flow" of our worldly popular culture. Teach me how to devote myself to You and Your Word and to apply Your principles to my life, so I can make a real difference for You. Thank You that as I take advantage of every opportunity that comes my way, You will use me to touch and change the lives of multitudes!

Not Perfect? Read This!

It is clear, then, that God's promise to give the whole earth to Abraham and his descendants was not because Abraham obeyed God's laws but because he trusted God to keep his promise. So if you still claim that God's blessings go to those who are "good enough," then you are saying that God's promises to those who have faith are meaningless, and faith is foolish. But the fact of the matter is this: when we try to gain God's blessing and salvation by keeping his laws we always end up under his anger, for we always fail to keep them. The only way we can keep from breaking laws is not to have any to break! So God's blessings are given to us by faith, as a free gift.

ROMANS 4:13-16 TLB

When I first saw these verses in the Bible, I underlined them and put stars all around them. Do you ever feel like you don't deserve God's gift of salvation? If you do, I know how you feel. These verses are for you as much as for me. They tell us that we don't have to earn salvation or God's love. We couldn't even if we wanted to. The truth is, we could never be "good enough" to save ourselves. That's exactly why God sent us a Savior. In fact, the Bible reveals that even our best efforts wouldn't measure up. Isaiah 64:6 says, "All our righteous acts are like filthy rags." But while we can't model perfection, we can model spiritual growth. Out of gratitude for God's gracious gift, we can seek to abide in Him and be fruitful for His glory. And we can serve Him and others out of a thankful heart.

In Ephesians 2:8-9, Paul writes, "For it is by grace you have been saved, through faith—and this not from yourselves, it is the gift of God—not by works, so that no one can boast." One reason why God wants to make our salvation a gift is so that we can't boast about it or take the credit for it. God wants the glory, and He deserves it. Scripture reveals that when people asked Jesus, "What must we do to do the works God requires?" He answered them, "The work of God is this: to believe in the one he has sent" (John 6:28,29). We all know how much Jesus spoke about the importance of our doing good works and loving and serving God, but here He gives us the bottom line. It's not what we do that matters most to God; it's in whom we believe. It's not what we do that makes us righteous in God's sight; it's what He has done for us. Does that mean that the Bible condones sin? Not at all. The same man who wrote the verses above in Romans 4, the apostle Paul, also wrote in Romans 6:2, "Shall we go on sinning so that grace may increase? By no means! We died to sin; how can we live in it any longer?" From the moment of salvation, we are empowered

LIVE ON PURPOSE TODAY

Spend a few moments today rejoicing in your free gift of salvation, serving God out of a thankful heart!

by the Holy Spirit to resist sin and obey God. We become increasingly uncomfortable with sin, and God's ways become more attractive to us. And Scripture assures us that "God is at work within us, helping us want to obey him, and then helping us do what he wants" (Phil. 2:13 TLB). I pray that these truths will help you to relax a little more and enjoy your special relationship with God. May you rest in this precious promise from Him: "So now, since we have been made right in God's sight by faith in his promises, we can have real peace with him because of what Jesus Christ our Lord has done for us"! (Rom. 5:1 TLB).

PRAYER

Lord, forgive me for trying to earn the salvation You want me to receive as a free gift. Help me to stop striving to please You and to learn to abide and rest in You. Give me a revelation of my new identity in Christ so that I can cooperate with Your plan for my spiritual growth. Thank You for showing me that it's not my perfection that counts, but Yours!

From Trials to Triumphs

About midnight Paul and Silas were praying and singing
hymns to God, and the other prisoners were listening to them.
Suddenly there was such a violent earthquake that the
foundations of the prison were shaken. At once all the prison
doors flew open, and everybody's chains came loose.

ACTS 16:25,26

Paul and Silas were thrown into prison in Philippi for casting a demon out of a young slave girl who had been earning her master a lot of money. The disciples were stripped, beaten, and chained in a cell. The next thing that happened still amazes me, no matter how often I read it in Scripture. Paul and Silas began to pray and praise God in song. Most of us would have been grumbling and drowning in self-pity. We might have said something like, "God, here I am trying to serve You and lead others to You. How could You let these people do this to me? I don't deserve this!" Fortunately, instead of complaining, these disciples praised God, who responded by miraculously setting His servants free from captivity. As a result, the jailer and his entire household became believers.

Perhaps you are in a trial of your own today. Maybe the last thing you feel like doing is praising God. But listen to what Scripture teaches us. David said in Psalm 34:1, "I will bless the Lord at all times; his praise shall continually be in my mouth." And he meant it. Whether David was experiencing good times or bad, he praised God. Just one example of this is in 2 Samuel

LIVE ON PURPOSE TODAY

Whether you're experiencing an "up" or a "down"—and even if it's midnight in your circumstances—stop right now and offer up thanksgiving, praise, and worship to the Lord!

12:20, where David and Bathsheba's infant son has just died as part of God's chastisement of the couple. The first thing David does is "go into the house of the Lord and worship God." This is just one of the many reasons why God called David a man after His own heart. And though the Lord allowed His servant to suffer the consequences of his sins, He gave David victory over all his enemies and blessed him with great wealth and honor. Paul and Silas praised God in the darkest of circumstances and unbelievers turned to Christ. If you'll praise God in your trials, your example could very well attract the attention of those who won't be reached any other way. Not only that, but you may find that the Lord will turn your trials into triumphs!

PRAYER

Lord, forgive me for the times I've grumbled and felt sorry for myself in times of trouble. I ask You to remind me that You deserve praise through all my ups and downs. Help me to realize how blessed I really am, and give me a thankful heart. Thank You that my example will change the lives of others for Your glory!

Faithful in Little Things

He who is faithful in a very little thing is faithful also in much.

LUKE 16:10 NASB

Unless you are faithful in small matters,
you won't be faithful in large ones.

LUKE 16:10 NLT

When my son Joseph was a junior in high school, he felt led to attend the "See You at the Pole" event for the first time. It was his heart's desire to join fellow Christian students and teachers who gathered around their school flagpole to pray and praise the Lord. But when the actual morning arrived, Joseph was having second thoughts about attending because he was so gripped by fear that he felt sick to his stomach. After we sought God in prayer, Joseph "set his face like flint" and took his place next to all the other believers gathered at his school in the Lord's name. My son met a lot of wonderful new Christian friends that day, and they discussed the possibility of starting a Bible club and holding weekly meetings on campus for Bible study and prayer. The Lord gave me a burden to pray for this club to become a reality, even though there had never been a successful one in the history of the school. Weeks turned into months without any sign of a club forming, but I persevered in prayer. Then Joseph shared with me how he felt that God was calling him to approach the school authorities about starting weekly meetings. As he began the process of securing permission to launch a Bible club on campus, the Lord opened one door after another and our dream became a reality. Under Joseph's leadership and the subsequent leadership of my younger son, John, this club touched and changed the lives of a multitude of students from our community and many others.

When I was praying for a high school Bible club, it never occurred to me that the Lord would use my own son to start it. Many of the other Christian students had been believers a lot longer than my son, and in many ways, he lacked their spiritual maturity. Nevertheless, God chose Joseph and used him in awesome ways for His glory. I have no doubts that Joseph's attendance at the "See You at the Pole" event that day had everything to do with the Lord choosing him to launch and lead the club. And I also believe that my faithfulness in prayer for the club was linked to God's choosing my own son to start it. In addition, the Lord blessed me with some of the most exciting and rewarding years of my life by making me the "Club Mom." As my family and I have walked with God over the years, He has taught us how one small act of obedience on our part can lead to major blessings. Many people are waiting for a "big event" in order to obey God. What they fail to realize is that if they don't obey Him in small matters, their "big event" may never come. Jesus said, "Unless you are faithful in small matters, you won't be

LIVE ON PURPOSE TODAY

Surely as you read these words, little things God is asking of you began to pop into your mind. Make note of them with paper and pen, and then endeavor to demonstrate faithfulness to the Lord by checking off as many as possible before the sun goes down.

faithful in large ones" (Luke 16:10 NLT). Make no mistake—before the Lord will use us to make a difference in this world, we will be tested. We will have to prove to God that He can count on us to obey Him in seemingly insignificant matters, simply because He's the One doing the talking. The truth is that no job that He assigns us is insignificant in His sight. When the Lord leads us "just" to pray for someone or about something, we are partnering with Him just as much as when we're performing a task that brings us considerable recognition. You can bet that when God gives us a seemingly small matter to attend to, Satan will try to convince us that how we respond won't make any difference. He will try to get us to take our obedience casually. This is just one of the many tactics the enemy uses to try to keep us from fulfilling our God-given purpose. I encourage you to begin praying today that the Lord will make you sensitive and obedient to His voice, even in the smallest of matters. Rest assured that heartfelt prayers like these will open the door for God to fill your life with more purpose and meaning than you ever dreamed possible!

PRAYER

Lord, give me a new awareness of how important it is for me to obey You even in the smallest of matters. Make me sensitive and obedient to Your voice, and give me discernment to recognize the voice of the enemy. Don't let me miss out on Your perfect plans for my life. Thank You for making me faithful in little things so that I can be faithful also in much!

Keeping Our Dreams in Proper Perspective

Each one should use whatever gift he has received to serve others, faithfully administering God's grace in its various forms. If anyone serves, he should do it with the strength God provides, so that in all things God may be praised through Jesus Christ.

1 PETER 4:10,11

Several years ago I saw a famous Christian singer being interviewed on television. She was talking about how she had always wanted to reach millions for Christ with her musical talents and to glorify God with her popularity. Then she said something that really made an impression on me, and that has stuck with me till this day. She said that she decided long ago that if the Lord didn't allow her dream to be fulfilled, she would just depend on Him to give her the grace to deal with it—and she would go on and enjoy her life just the same. What I admired most about this young woman was that she had the faith and the courage to put her dreams and desires "on the altar," and to leave them in God's hands. She admitted that she would have been sorely disappointed if her dreams didn't come to pass, but she refused to have a "do or die" attitude about her heartfelt desires, and she surrendered them to the Lord.

There's nothing wrong with having visions, dreams, and goals. God wants us to have these things. But He wants us to have goals that line up with His will for us. When we get into agreement with God's will and purposes for our lives, there's no devil in hell, no person on earth, that can stop them from coming to pass. In fact, the only one who can really stand between us and our God-given destiny is us. Satan can't. Our families can't. Our bosses can't. Even the government can't. No one can prevent us from becoming the man or woman of God that we were created to be. Except us. We can live our lives the way we want to, and we can turn our backs on God's perfect plans for us, if we so choose. And in the end, all we will have to show for it is regret. Or we can get in line with God's will for us, and we can watch Him unfold our lives like a beautiful flower, one petal at a time. We can do this by surrendering ourselves to the Lord—spirit, soul, and body—and by seeking Him and His will for us every day of our lives through prayer, devotion, and the study of His Word.

One thing I've learned from walking with the Lord these ten years is this—God will test our devotion to Him by letting us experience times of disappointment, especially where the fulfillment of our dreams is concerned. How we respond to these disappointments will help determine how much God can use us and bless us. If we respond with pouting, sulking, complaining, or threatening, God will have to treat us like the babies we're imitating, and He will not be able to trust us with the level of responsibility or blessing He longs to. But if we respond with an attitude that says—"God, I don't understand this, and it really hurts, but I believe that You are good, and You will work this out

LIVE ON PURPOSE TODAY

Verbalize to yourself—or perhaps to a spouse or best friend—new directions the Lord is speaking to your heart. Also share with this confidant how you will keep the Lord in first place as you pursue new direction.

for my good"—the Lord will reward our faithfulness and spiritual maturity beyond our highest expectations. I recently heard a definition for *idol* that made me shudder. It said, "An idol is anything you feel you can't live without and be happy." It can be a dream, a desire, a thing, or even a person. The Bible says that our God is a jealous God, and He's not about to share us with anything or anyone else. (Ex. 20:5.) He expects our wholehearted devotion, and He deserves it, simply because He's God. If we ever find ourselves desiring something so much that we feel we can't live without it, God may close the door to it—either temporarily or permanently—depending on what He feels is best for our spiritual well-being. The Lord wants us to be able to say with all sincerity, "God, I can live without this dream—but I can't live without *You!*" With an attitude like this, we can walk in the awesome plans and purposes that God has mapped out for us, and we can have all the joy, peace, and fulfillment that are ours in Christ.

If God has closed a door on a heartfelt desire or dream of yours today, take comfort in the fact that He is saying to you one of two things. Either it's, "Wait. It's not the right time yet." Or, "I have something better for you." In either case, you can't lose, because you have put your trust in a God who loves you with a perfect love, and who has your best interests at heart!

PRAYER

Lord, show me Your will and purposes for my life, and help me to make them my personal goals. Help me to always give You first place in my life so that everything else will fall into place. When I experience disappointment and heartache, comfort me and fill me with a fresh sense of hope. I can live without the things of this world, Lord—but I can't live without You!

A Message of Restoration

{ *I will repay you for the years the locusts have eaten...*
and you will praise the name of the Lord your
God who has worked wonders for you. }

JOEL 2:25,26

These verses in the Bible have special meaning for me because I didn't become serious about my relationship with God until I was almost 40 years old. There have been many times when I've lamented over the fact that my children weren't raised in a true Christian home from the time they were born. And I've often regretted that my relationship with my husband and our marriage didn't get off on the right foot because of our lack of devotion to the Lord from the very beginning. If I allowed myself to dwell on things like these, I could come up with a multitude of regrets. Thankfully, God gave me these verses as a personal promise that He would work wonders for me by restoring the blessings I forfeited during all those years I was living for myself instead of Him. And He's been true to His Word. As I live this new life in Christ daily, I am continually amazed by the marvelous works of restoration that the Lord performs for me and my loved ones on a regular basis.

If you'll ask the Lord to reveal Himself to you as the God of restoration, He will restore things in your life that you thought were lost forever. I've seen Him restore broken families and relationships. I've also seen Him breathe new life into lost dreams and visions. And I've witnessed His miraculous power working in

LIVE ON PURPOSE TODAY

As God begins the work of restoration in your life, begin to pick up things you thought were lost forever—goals, dreams, talents, even friendships and relationships. As the Holy Spirit guides you, demonstrate fervor as if not even one day had slipped by.

people's lives to restore their health and finances. But I think the things He restores that mean the most to me are our faith, joy, peace, and hope. The Bible makes it abundantly clear—our God is in the restoration business. And my life and the lives of many others are living proof. If you're a child of the King, you don't have to assume that all the losses that come your way are set in stone. If you'll give the Lord a chance to have the final word, you'll be amazed at what He can do to make your whole life shiny and new!

PRAYER

Lord, today I believe and receive Your precious promises of restoration. I ask that You work wonders in my life by transforming my losses into blessings. Help me to do my part by seeking You daily and putting my trust in You. Thank You for making my whole life bright and beautiful for Your glory!

Cast Those Cares

Cast your cares on the Lord and he will sustain you;
he will never let the righteous fall.

PSALM 55:22

"**S**ustain" is a great word. If you look it up in the dictionary, the definition says: "To provide for the support of; specifically to provide sustenance or nourishment for; carry the weight or burden of."[4] God is promising us in the verse above that if we will do our part by casting our cares upon Him, He will do His part by sustaining us. I think that's a pretty good deal, don't you? But let's be honest here. Casting our cares on the Lord isn't always as easy as it sounds. Even when we sincerely want to hand our burdens over to God, we often can't. Many times we're left struggling with burdens God never meant for us to handle. The results are often anxiety, depression, despair, and even sickness and infirmity. But maybe I can help convince you that God really does want to carry your burdens, and that it's worth the effort to surrender them to Him. In 1 Peter 5:7 NLT, the apostle Peter restates the verse above: "Give all your worries and cares to God, for he cares about what happens to you." It's because God cares—and because He never created you to shoulder your burdens alone—that He wants you to give Him all your worries. Only God's shoulders are big enough to carry our daily concerns. Ours aren't. Look at this promise in Psalm 68:19: "Praise be to the Lord, to God our Savior, who daily bears our burdens." All these verses make it clear that God wants to bear *all* our cares *all* the time.

In Luke 21:34-35 TLB, Jesus gives us this stern warning: "Watch out! Don't let my sudden coming catch you unaware; don't let me find you…occupied with the problems of this life, like all the rest of the world." And in Mark 4:19, Jesus says that "the worries of this life" can actually "choke the word [of God], making it unfruitful" in our lives. Instead, the Savior tells us, "Come to me, all of you who are weary and carry heavy burdens, and I will give you rest. Take my yoke upon you. Let me teach you, because I am humble and gentle, and you will find rest for your souls. For my yoke fits perfectly, and the burden I give you is light" (Matt. 11:28-30 NLT). If we let the Savior teach us His way of handling the affairs of this life, we will find the rest and relief He so graciously offers. It's the Lord's sincere desire that we give all our cares to Him, but He won't wrestle them away from us. We must surrender them to Him, trusting that He has our

LIVE ON PURPOSE TODAY

Cast your cares on the Lord today in a way you won't soon forget. Stretch one hand out in front of you. With the other hand, imagine that you pick up your care and deposit it in the outstretched hand. Now, hand it up to the Lord—and be done with it once and for all!

best interests at heart. When we do, we open the door for God to work wonders in our circumstances and lives. Each day, tell the Lord, "I give You all my cares and burdens, Lord. Thank You for sustaining me, according to Your promise." You can be specific, naming your cares if you want to. Then when worry or doubt come against you, say, "Lord, I thank You that You're taking care of that for me!" And let the peace of God quiet your heart and mind. May this precious promise from God encourage you today:

"I will be your God through all your lifetime, yes, even when your hair is white with age. I made you and I will care for you. I will carry you along and be your Savior"! (Isa. 46:4 TLB).

PRAYER

Lord, today I cast all my cares upon You. When I'm tempted to carry my own burdens, remind me that Your will is for me to surrender them to You. Give me a new awareness of Your ability and willingness to solve my problems and handle my affairs. Thank You for rewarding me with rest and relief!

The Power of Joy

*Don't be dejected and sad, for the joy
of the Lord is your strength!*

NEHEMIAH 8:10 NLT

When I was going through a very difficult time recently and praying for strength, the Lord showed me the above verse. I had read it countless times before, but this time it shed new light on a simple truth for me. In order for us to be truly strong in spirit, the way God wants us to be, we must be filled with His joy. If you don't believe this is true, the next time you begin to feel weak or weary, check your joy level. Chances are that it will be way down. The kind of joy I'm speaking about is not the worldly "feel good" kind, but it's a deep, abiding joy born of the Holy Spirit. The Bible says that joy is a fruit of the Spirit. (Gal. 5:22.) All believers have the "seed" of joy planted in our spirits, and it's up to us to cooperate with God to develop it and help it grow. One way we can do that is by praying for joy. Once I began reading the Scriptures and discovering that I had a God-given right to be filled with His joy, I began praying for it confidently, based on 1 John 5:14-15, which says that when we pray according to the will of God, we will receive what we ask for. David confirms that praying for joy is scriptural when he writes, "Bring joy to Your servant, for to You, O Lord, I lift up my soul" (Ps. 86:4).

Jesus said that answered prayer can be a source of joy. He tells us, "Ask, using My name, and you will receive, and your cup of joy will overflow" (John 16:24). I have found that the more I pray, the more blessings I receive and the more my joy abounds. Another way to cultivate the seed of joy in us is to encourage ourselves with God's truth and promises. Psalm 119:162 says, "I rejoice in Your promise like one who finds great spoil." Some translations say "great treasure." If you've ever gone through a trial and had nothing to hang on to but a promise from God, like I have, you know how precious His Word can be and how much joy it can bring to a troubled heart. Spending time in God's presence is another way of increasing our joy. David wrote, "You will fill me with joy in Your presence" (Ps. 16:11). There's simply no substitute for spending time with God in prayer, praise, and Bible reading. That's when He imparts to us His wisdom, peace, joy, and strength. When we neglect to spend quality time with God, our burdens become unbearable and our joy diminishes.

Jesus made it clear that joy was God's will for us. He said that He wanted the "full measure" of His joy to be in us (John 17:13). And He said that He desired that our joy would be "complete" (John 15:11). The Savior wasn't talking about a fleeting sense of happiness here, but one that would endure in the face of adversity. That's why He told us, "Here on earth you will have many trials and sorrows; but cheer up, for I have overcome the world" (John 16:33 TLB). The Amplified Bible goes on to say, "I have deprived it of power to harm you and have conquered it for

LIVE ON PURPOSE TODAY

Encourage yourself with God's truth and promises today. In fact, double up on your time in the Bible—it's guaranteed to stir up your joy and put a smile on your face!

you." He also said, "No one will take away your joy" (John 16:22). Jesus has made a way for us to have the joy of the Lord in a trouble-filled world. But it's up to us to do our part by nurturing our joy and by refusing to surrender it to the enemy. Satan works overtime trying to steal our joy because he knows that it makes us strong and difficult to defeat. He also knows that he can seriously damage our witness and our effectiveness as believers if he can keep us sad, sour, and sullen.

Maybe you've heard the old saying, "Laughter is the best medicine." There's actually a scriptural basis for this truth. Proverbs 17:22 NASB says, "A joyful heart is good medicine." Even much of today's scientific and medical community will acknowledge that there is a direct connection between our joy level and our health and well-being. The Bible says that we should be "filled with an inexpressible and glorious joy" as the result of our faith in Jesus and our love for Him (1 Peter 1:8 NIV). God deserves cheerful servants, and it should be our goal to worship and serve Him with joy. (Ps. 100:2.) Finally, nothing brings more joy to our hearts than placing our wholehearted trust in God, especially in times of trouble. (Rom. 15:13.) If you are facing challenging circumstances today and have lost your joy in the Lord, you may be handing your blessings and your well-being over to the enemy on a silver platter. Don't do it. Hang on to your joy till the victory comes, trusting that the Lord's strength will be there for you every step of the way!

PRAYER

Lord, fill me with Your joy to give me strength. Show me how to have the kind of joy that draws others to You. When the enemy comes against me and I'm tempted to lose my joy, remind me of what it can cost me. Thank You that Your joy shall remain in me and overflow!

Breaking Destructive Patterns

{
People ruin their lives by their own foolishness and then are angry at the Lord.

PROVERBS 19:3 NLT
}

I recently heard from a woman who complained about all of the men she had been in relationship with who had lied, cheated, and mistreated her. She was completely disgusted, and she sounded bitter and resentful. She asked for prayer, that God would finally send her a decent man who she could share her life with and who would be good to her. As I read her words, it didn't take long for me to figure out what this woman's real problem was. It wasn't men, in general. And it wasn't God. It was her. This woman was continually being hurt because she was continually out of God's will, where her relationships were concerned. She was not being led by God's Spirit in choosing a partner, but she was being led by her own feelings and emotions. And as a result, her relationships with these men were doomed to fail.

Maybe you've known people like this woman. I certainly have. And maybe, like me, you've desperately tried to help them. Unfortunately, people like these who have displayed a pattern of failed relationships and destructive habits aren't likely to change just because we reach out to them. Scripture says, "A short-tempered man must bear his own penalty; you can't do much to help him. If you must try once, you must try a dozen times!" (Prov. 19:19 TLB). While this proverb refers to people who have a habit of losing their temper, the principle is the same for those who exhibit other destructive tendencies. Another proverb puts it like this: "As a dog returns to his vomit, so a fool repeats his folly" (Prov. 26:11 NLT). We can earnestly pray for these people, and we can give them sound advice when the Lord leads us to, but anything beyond that will most likely be a waste of time and energy on our part. What these people really need is a change of heart, and that's something that can only come from God. Sadly, God is often the last one that people like these will resort to.

LIVE ON PURPOSE TODAY

The Lord will surely answer your request and reveal to you destructive patterns in your life and how to gain freedom. As He does, search God's Word for Scriptures that promise freedom from your destructive ways and meditate wholly upon them. They will bring you the strength to forge a new path.

What if *you* can identify with this woman yourself? I believe I have some godly advice for you today. First, focus on becoming the man or woman of God that you were created to be. The Lord is more likely to reward you with a loving and faithful mate if you are the kind of person who deserves such blessings from Him. Proverbs says, "The man who finds a wife finds a good thing; she is a blessing to him from the Lord" (Prov. 18:22 TLB). God may have the perfect spouse all picked out for you, but He may first want to prepare you to receive this blessed relationship so that it has every chance of not only surviving, but thriving, when you finally come together. Use this period of waiting to nurture your relationship with God. Jesus said, "Seek first His kingdom and His righteousness, and all these things will be given to you as well" (Matt. 6:33). Putting God first in our lives can have a positive impact on every area of our lives, even where our relationships are concerned. Second, trust God to bring the right mate for you at just the right time. Most people don't realize how critical this is, and because of that, they get involved with relationships that God never meant for them to. Realize that by involving yourself in the wrong relationships, you could be delaying or forfeiting the ideal one that God has destined for you.

Benjamin Franklin said, "The definition of insanity is doing the same thing over and over and expecting different results." When we've established a pattern that isn't working, we can call on the Lord to help us break that destructive pattern once and for all. When we do, we can rest assured that all the help of heaven will be on our side!

PRAYER

Lord, do a new work in my heart and life now so that I will begin to focus on becoming all You created me to be. Help me to wholeheartedly trust You to bring the right relationships into my life at just the right time. Please reveal to me any destructive patterns that I might have in my life today, and show me how to gain the freedom that is mine in Christ. Thank You, Lord, that no matter how badly I've failed in the past, I can begin to walk in victory as I give You first place in my life!

Endnotes

[1] *Webster's New World*™, *College Dictionary,* 3d. ed. (New York: Macmillian, 1996 Simon & Schuster), s.v. "procrastinate."

[2] *Webster's New World*™, 3d. ed., s.v. "tear."

[3] *Webster's New World*™, 3d. ed., s.v. "self-pity."

[4] *Webster's New World*™, 3d. ed., s.v. "sustain."

Prayer of Salvation

God loves you—no matter who you are, no matter what your past. God loves you so much that He gave His one and only begotten Son for you. The Bible tells us that "...whoever believes in him shall not perish but have eternal life" (John 3:16). Jesus laid down His life and rose again so that we could spend eternity with Him in heaven and experience His absolute best on earth. If you would like to receive Jesus into your life, say the following prayer out loud and mean it from your heart.

Heavenly Father, I come to You admitting that I am a sinner. Right now, I choose to turn away from sin, and I ask You to cleanse me of all unrighteousness. I believe that Your Son, Jesus, died on the cross to take away my sins. I also believe that He rose again from the dead so that I might be forgiven of my sins and made righteous through faith in Him. I call upon the name of Jesus Christ to be the Savior and Lord of my life. Jesus, I choose to follow You and ask that You fill me with the power of the Holy Spirit. I declare that right now I am a child of God. I am free from sin and full of the righteousness of God. I am saved in Jesus' name. Amen.

If you prayed this prayer to receive Jesus Christ as your Savior for the first time, please contact us on the Web at **www.harrisonhouse.com** to receive a free book.

Or you may write to us at
Harrison House
P.O. Box 35035
Tulsa, Oklahoma 74153

About the Author

J. M. Farro, gifted writer and author, reaches out to thousands of people through **www.jesus freakhideout.com**. Since 1996, this popular web site has grown in scope and outreach beyond the boundaries of the Christian music industry.
Their focus is album reviews, artist information, interviews, music news, and ministry through devotionals and prayer. On staff since 1998, J. M. Farro counsels thousands of men and women around the globe each year through her devotionals and prayer ministry. She and her husband, Joe, have two sons. They make their home in Nazareth, Pennsylvania.

To contact J.M. Farro, please write to:

J. M. Farro
P.O. Box 434
Nazareth, PA 18064

Or you may email her at:
farro@jesusfreakhideout.com
or jmf@jmfarro.com

Please include your prayer requests and comments when you write.

Other Books by J.M. Farro

Life on Purpose™ Devotional for Women
Life on Purpose™ Devotional for Men

www.harrisonhouse.com

Fast. Easy. Convenient!

- ◆ New Book Information
- ◆ Look Inside the Book
- ◆ Press Releases
- ◆ Bestsellers

- ◆ Free E-News
- ◆ Author Biographies
- ◆ Upcoming Books
- ◆ Share Your Testimony

For the latest in book news and author information, please visit us on the Web at www.harrisonhouse.com. Get up-to-date pictures and details on all our powerful and life-changing products. Sign up for our e-mail newsletter, *Friends of the House,* and receive free monthly information on our authors and products including testimonials, author announcements, and more!

Harrison House—
Books That Bring Hope, Books That Bring Change

The Harrison House Vision

Proclaiming the truth and the power

Of the Gospel of Jesus Christ

With excellence;

Challenging Christians to

Live victoriously,

Grow spiritually,

Know God intimately.